50 Deliciously Decorative Cookies

50 Deliciously
Decorative Cookies

Easy-to-Make Cookie Creations

Fiona Pearce

ST. MARTIN'S GRIFFIN
NEW YORK

A QUARTO BOOK

50 Deliciously Decorative Cookies

Copyright © 2014 Quarto Inc.
Printed in China. For information, address
St. Martin's Press, 175 Fifth Avenue,
New York, N.Y. 10010.

www.stmartins.com

Library of Congress Cataloging-in-Publication Data
Available Upon Request

ISBN: 978-1-250-05210-0

St. Martin's Griffin books may be purchased for
educational, business, or promotional use. For
information on bulk purchases, please contact
Macmillan Corporate and Premium Sales
Department at 1-800-221-7945, extension 5442,
or write specialmarkets@macmillan.com

First U.S. Edition: November 2014

QUAR.DCOO

Conceived, designed, and produced by:
Quarto Publishing plc
The Old Brewery
6 Blundell Street
London N7 9BH

Senior Editor: Ruth Patrick
Designer: Karin Skånberg
Photographer: Sian Irvine
Food and Prop Stylist: Fiona Pearce
Proofreader: Sarah Hoggett
Indexer: Helen Snaith
Art Director: Caroline Guest
Creative Director: Moira Clinch
Publisher: Paul Carslake

Color separation in Singapore
by PICA Digital Pte. Ltd.
Printed by 1010 Printing
International Ltd, China

9 8 7 6 5 4 3 2 1

Contents

Fiona's World of Cookies

Whether it's a gift to say thank you, or a sweet little treat
to celebrate a special event, pretty cookie creations always delight.

This book features over 50 projects, each with detailed step-by-step instructions and photographs to allow you to create beautiful cookies that can be adapted for any occasion. From a whimsical, three-dimensional birdhouse, to sophisticated cookies adorned with elegantly piped flourishes, or pretty charm cookies for children to string together to make edible accessories, the wide range of projects will provide you with endless hours of cookie-decorating fun.

I have arranged the projects into chapters according to the main decorating medium used—fondant, colored dough, edible icing sheets, royal icing, wafer paper, and chocolate—so you can easily find cookies to decorate based on the materials you have available. I encourage you to adapt the featured designs and experiment with different colors and shapes to make your creations unique. Don't make your cookie decorating about chasing perfection. Learn from your mistakes, adapt techniques, and above all, always have fun and be proud of what you make.

Although the book focuses on decorating techniques, my favorite tried-and-tested cookie and icing recipes are also included, so you can be sure that your cookies will taste as amazing as they look. My cookie recipes have been developed to ensure that the cookies don't spread and lose their shape during baking. But, it is perfectly fine to use your own recipes, or to even use store-bought plain cookies if you don't fancy baking or have little time. Remember, any plain cookie is a perfect blank canvas for decorating.

So, what are you waiting for? Grab your piping bag and let's get decorating!

Fiona
xx

A note on quantities

The amount of fondant, royal icing, or chocolate (or candy wafers) you need for each project depends on the size of the cookies you would like to decorate, how thick you would like the fondant covering to be, and how many cookies you have made in a batch, so the project instructions do not specify an amount. Fondant is commercially available in various-sized packs. On average, an 8¾ oz (250 g) pack should be enough to cover at least 12–15 cookies (up to 3 in. (7.5 cm) in width). Any leftover fondant should be wrapped tightly in plastic wrap and stored at room temperature for future use. An 8¾ oz (250 g) batch of royal icing (see recipe on page 133) can be thinned down with water to flood the surface of at least 24 cookies. Any leftover royal icing that has not been thinned down can be stored in a refrigerator for up to 5 days. Chocolate and candy wafers come in different weights. On average, a 12 oz (340 g) bag of candy wafers is more than enough, once melted, to cover at least 24 cookies. Any leftover unmelted chocolate or candy wafers should be stored at room temperature in a resealable bag to retain freshness. You can also reuse leftover melted chocolate. Allow the chocolate to set at room temperature, then transfer it to a bag until you are ready to remelt it again.

Royal icing safety note

If you're decorating cookies for children, pregnant women, or anyone with compromised immune systems, you can use meringue powder instead of raw egg whites. Mix 5 tablespoons meringue powder with 1 lb (450 g) confectioners' sugar and a scant 4 fl oz (125 ml) of water to achieve stiff-peak royal icing.

Cookie Selector

On these pages you will find the cookies featured in the book. Browse the selector to find the design that would work best for the occasion, then turn to the instructions on the referenced page.

Colored
Dough
page 48

Royal Icing
page 68

Continued next page

Strawberry Baskets
page 92

Charm Bracelets
page 94

Marbled Flowers
page 96

Wafer
Paper
page 106

Whimsical
Water Lilies
page 108

Perfume Bottles
page 110

Frilly Lace Fancies
page 112

Pretty as a Picture
page 114

Quick Cookie
Creations
page 126

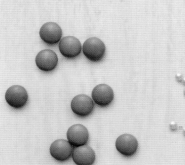

Cookie
and Icing
Recipes
page 130

Recipes
page 130

Tools & Equipment

There are endless decorating tools available to buy, but here are a few items that are regularly used throughout this book and will be useful for any future cookie or cake decorating projects.

Basic equipment

To bake cookies, you don't need many more specialist pieces of equipment than you would for other bakes. It's likely that you'll have most of the basic equipment needed to bake the cookies featured in this book hiding in your kitchen.

1. Palette knife for lifting dough and fondant.

2. Non-stick rolling pins for rolling out cookie dough, fondant, and gum paste.

3. Parchment paper for lining baking sheets.

4. Wire cooling rack to let cookies cool on once baked before decorating.

5. Baking sheet for baking cookies on.

6. Large non-stick board on which to roll out fondant and gum paste.

7. Cookie cutters to cut out cookie dough and fondant into different shapes.

8. Cookie sticks to insert into cookies before baking to make cookie pops.

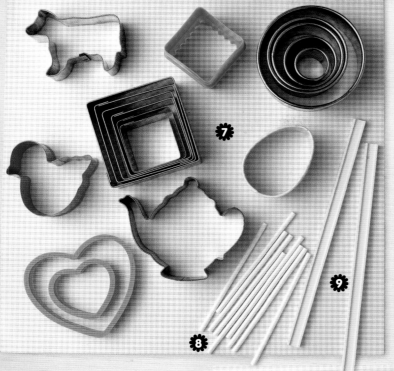

9. Spacers to roll out cookie dough or fondant to an even thickness.

10. Squeeze bottles filled with thinned royal icing to flood the surface of a cookie.

11. Piping bags to fill with royal icing.

12. Paintbrushes (range of thicknesses) for dusting and gluing decorations and for brush embroidery.

13. Paint palette for mixing edible paints and dusts and shaping decorations.

14. Scissors to cut out edible icing sheets and wafer paper.

15. Paste colors to color icing and cookie dough.

16. Edible glue for attaching decorations to cookies.

17. Decorating tips for piping royal icing.

18. Piping gel to attach a fondant covering on cookies.

19. Electric mixer to mix the cookie dough and royal icing.

Decorating tools

There is an endless amount of specialist decorating equipment available online and in cake decorating supply stores. You can always start by getting a few tools and then, over time, collect more equipment as your skills develop and as you wish to try the more elaborate designs featured in some of the projects.

1. Cake smoother to smooth the top of fondant on cookies.

2. Quilting tool to emboss fondant with a stitching effect.

3. Ball tool for shaping decorations.

4. Scribing tool for making outlines in cookies before decorating.

5. Bone tool for thinning and shaping the edge of gum paste decorations.

6. Veiner tool for adding a vein pattern or frilling petals.

7. Patchwork cutters for cutting out decorations or embossing fondant.

8. Embossing stamps and mats for adding patterns or texture to fondant.

9. Plunger cutters for making decorations such as blossoms in fondant and gum paste.

10. Shaped cutters (metal and plastic varieties) for cutting out shapes such as leaves, flowers, and geometric shapes in fondant and gum paste.

11. Stencils to add patterns to cookies with dusts or royal icing.

12. Paper punch for cutting designs and shapes in wafer paper.

13. Rubber stamps for printing patterns with edible ink onto cookies.

14. Veining molds for adding texture to molded flowers.

15. Silicone molds for making decorations such as cameos and bows with fondant or gum paste, or for shaping cookie dough before baking.

16. Cookie mold to make chocolate-covered Oreo cookies in different designs.

17. Foam pad to cushion decorations as they are being shaped and frilled.

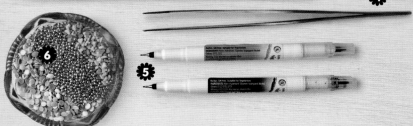

Decorating materials

Freshly baked cookies are delicious on their own, but they can be made extra special by decorating them. There are lots of different edible mediums that can be used to decorate cookies, including:

1. Chocolate transfer sheets to transfer colorful patterns onto chocolate to make decorations for cookies.

2. Edible icing sheets printed with a design that can be cut out and used on cookies or to make decorations.

3. Wafer paper to make edible, translucent decorations such as flowers.

4. Fondant to cover the tops of cookies or to make pretty decorations.

5. Candy wafers to make chocolate decorations.

6. Royal icing to flood the tops of cookies, attach decorations to cookies, or do fine piping work.

Finishing touches

Add a touch of glamour to your cookies by dusting them with edible glittery dusts or prettifying them with colored sugar or sprinkles. There are so many different colored edible decorations available that you will be spoilt for choice and can usually find any color to suit your cookie theme.

1. Edible luster dust to add definition to decorations, create paint, or use with a stencil to create patterns.

2. Sanding sugar to decorate or add texture to cookies.

3. Edible pearls to decorate cookies or make edible jewels.

4. Tweezers for adding edible pearls to cookies and decorations.

5. Edible pens to draw designs onto cookies.

6. Nonpareils or sprinkles to decorate or add texture to cookies.

Core Techniques

With a little practice to master some core techniques, baking and decorating beautiful cookies is within anyone's reach.

Baking Cookies

By following a few simple tips, you can ensure that your cookies are always baked to perfection.

9. Always bake cookies in a preheated oven. Try to bake cookies of a similar size on the same baking sheet so that they all require the same amount of time to bake. Smaller cookies don't take as long to bake as larger ones.

10. Be careful not to over-bake your cookies. Once they are ready, remove them from the baking sheet and allow them to cool completely on a wire rack. This will allow the steam to evaporate and your cookies will harden.

11. Undecorated cookies can be stored in an airtight container in the freezer for up to one month.

12. Most decorated cookies have about a two-week shelf life if stored at room temperature in an airtight container.

Method

1. Ensure that your cookie dough is chilled before you roll it out.

2. Roll out chilled dough on a lightly floured surface. It is important that you don't add too much flour to the dough while you are rolling it out, otherwise the cookies can become quite dry.

3. If your dough is quite sticky, place a piece of parchment paper over the top of it before rolling it out. This will make the dough easier to handle and will ensure that the dough does not stick to the rolling pin.

4. To ensure that the dough is rolled out to an even thickness, you can use a rolling pin with built-in guide rings or place ¼ in. (5 mm) spacers on either side of your dough. Make sure that your rolling pin sits across the top of both spacers while rolling. Use different-sized spacers to achieve thicker or thinner dough.

5. Once your dough is rolled out to the required thickness, you can use cookie cutters or a knife to cut out different shapes. If using cutters, dip them in flour before cutting out each shape to prevent the dough from sticking to them.

6. Try to cut your cookies as close together as possible to limit the amount of leftover dough. Although you can easily re-roll the remaining dough, each time you roll it out, the dough becomes slightly tougher and the texture of the cookies can change.

7. Once the cookie shapes are cut out, use a palette knife to carefully transfer them to a baking sheet lined with baking parchment. Make sure you leave room between the cookies on the baking sheet to allow them to expand a bit during baking.

8. Chill the cookies for at least 10 minutes in a freezer or 30 minutes in a refrigerator before baking them. This will help to prevent them spreading too much or changing shape during baking.

Royal icing can be used to create a smooth, hard covering for your cookies. Once the covering has dried, decorations can be added, or more royal icing can be piped on top.

Flooding Cookies with Royal Icing

To cover a cookie with royal icing, the surface of the cookie needs to be flooded with thinned icing. This can be achieved by following the steps on this page.

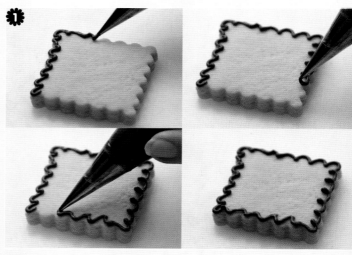

Method

1. Use medium-peak royal icing in a piping bag fitted with a No 2 round decorating tip to pipe around the edge of the cookie.

Tips

If your royal icing is too thick, add a few drops of water to it to dilute it. If your icing is too runny, adjust the consistency by adding a little confectioners' sugar.

*

Fill a squeeze bottle with thinned royal icing—this will make it easier to control the icing as it is added to the top of the cookie.

2. Apply thinned royal icing into the outlined section of the cookie to flood it with royal icing. Be careful not to overfill the cookie, otherwise the royal icing will leak over the edge of the outline.

3. You may need to use a toothpick to drag the royal icing toward the edges of the outline.

4. Sometimes air bubbles may appear in the royal icing, so have a pin or toothpick on hand to pop them.

5. Leave the cookies to dry for at least 4 hours (preferably overnight).

Ready-made fondant and gum paste are widely
available and come in many colors. However, you can
also make any color you require by adding edible food
coloring to white (uncolored) fondant or gum paste.

Coloring Icing

Liquid food colorings are usually not suitable
for coloring fondant or gum paste because they
can change the consistency of the icing, making
it sticky and difficult to work with. It is best to use
gel (concentrated) colorings and add the color
gradually until the desired color is achieved.

Method

1. Use a toothpick to add color
to fondant or gum paste. Dark
colors will need more coloring
than lighter shades.

2. Knead well until an even color
is achieved. If you accidentally add
too much color, knead in more
white fondant or gum paste to
achieve a lighter shade.

3. To prevent your hands from
being dyed when coloring fondant
or gum paste, it is advisable to
wear disposable gloves.

Fondant is a sweet, opaque icing that is soft, pliable and easily rolled, making it a very versatile medium for covering cookies or making pretty decorations.

Covering Cookies with Fondant

The steps on these pages will help you achieve a smooth fondant covering for your cookies.

Method

1. Knead the fondant well before use.

2. Use a non-stick rolling pin to roll out the fondant on a non-stick surface to approximately ⅛ in. (3 mm) in thickness.

3. Cut out a shape using the cookie cutter or template used to create the cookie. Roll the excess fondant into a ball and wrap it in plastic wrap so that you can use it later.

Fondant can also be used to make pretty decorations for your cookies (see page 28).

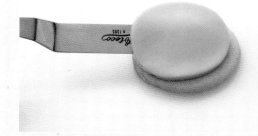

5. Carefully lift the fondant shape using a palette knife and place it on top of the cookie.

4. Paint the surface of a cookie with piping gel (or boiled jam), using a clean paintbrush. The piping gel will act as glue and ensure that the fondant sticks firmly to the cookie.

Tip

Smear a small amount of white vegetable fat (shortening) on your work surface to prevent the fondant from sticking to it.

Layers of fondant in different shapes and sizes are built up on the surface of the cookies to create the pretty Button Flowers (see page 24).

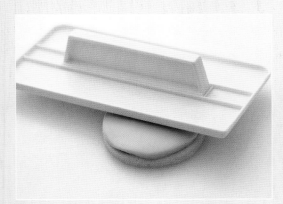

6. If you have accidentally put any fingerprints or marks on the fondant, use the palm of your hand or a cake smoother to gently polish the surface of the fondant to remove any blemishes.

7. To achieve a professional finish, gently rub a finger around the edge of the fondant to smooth any rough edges.

Fondant

Fondant is a sweet, opaque dough made from confectioners' sugar and glucose. It can be bought in a range of colors from cake decorating supply stores or online suppliers, or you can make your own (see recipes on pages 134–135). Decorating with fondant is the simplest way to create a pretty cookie in no time. It is easy to shape and you can add texture to it with embossing tools.

Button Flowers

Layer up different fondant cut-outs to make these cute flower cookies.

You will need

Materials: Round fluted-edge cookies (2 in. [5 cm] in diameter) • Fondant—bright pink, purple, turquoise, emerald green, yellow • Clear piping gel • Edible glue **Tools:** Non-stick rolling pin • Fluted circle cutter (2 in. [5 cm] in diameter) • Fine paintbrush • Palette knife • Small circle cutters (1½ in. [4 cm] and 1¼ in. [3 cm] in diameter) • Small carnation cutters • Silicone button mold

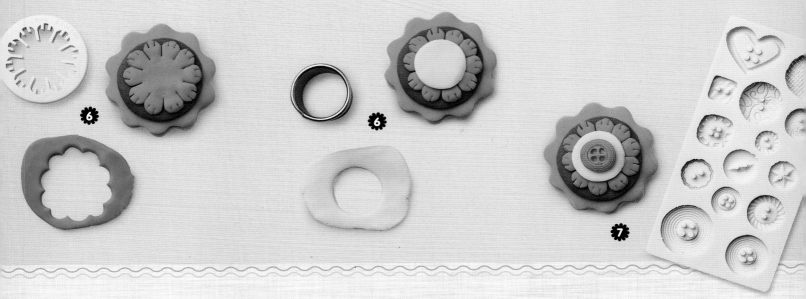

Method

1. Using a non-stick rolling pin, roll out the different-colored fondants on a non-stick surface to approximately ⅛ in. (3 mm) in thickness. Use the fluted circle cookie cutter to cut out fluted flower shapes.

2. Apply a thin layer of piping gel to the surface of each fluted cookie, using a fine paintbrush.

3. Carefully lift the fondant fluted flowers with a palette knife and place them on top of the cookies. The piping gel will act as glue and attach the fondant to the cookie.

4. Gently rub a finger around the edge of the fondant to achieve a smooth finish.

5. For each cookie, cut out 3 different-colored circles or flowers from the fondants, using small circle and carnation cutters. The cut-outs should all be different sizes and smaller than the cookie.

6. Begin to layer the 3 fondant cut-outs on top of the cookie, using edible glue to secure them in position. Place the largest cut out on the cookie first, finishing with the smallest.

7. Make a colored button for each flower by pressing fondant into a silicone button mold. Ensure the fondant is flush with the back of the mold, and then flex the mold gently to remove the button. Attach a button into the center of each flower cookie using edible glue.

Patchwork Blankets

Simple little square cookies that can be designed in any color scheme—they would make beautiful little gifts for a baby shower or christening.

You will need

Materials: Square cookies (2¾ in. [7 cm] in width) • Fondant—pale green, pale pink, yellow, lilac • Edible glue **Tools:** Non-stick rolling pin • Small square cutter (¾ in. [2 cm] in width) • Fine paintbrush • Palette knife • Selection of small embossing stamps and cutters • Quilting tool

Method

1. Using a non-stick rolling pin, roll out the colored fondants on a non-stick surface to approximately ⅛ in. (3 mm) in thickness. Use the small square cutter to cut out nine squares for each cookie. For my design, I have cut out at least 2 squares in each color, but you can use as few or as many colors as desired.

2. Apply a thin layer of edible glue to the surface of each cookie, using a fine paintbrush. Lift the fondant squares with a palette knife and place them on top of the cookies, in 3 rows of 3.

3. Gently rub a finger over the top and around the edge of the fondant to achieve a smooth finish and blend the edges of the squares together.

4. Press different embossing stamps and small cutters gently into each square to imprint a pattern into the fondant. It is important to do this while the fondant is still fresh, otherwise it will crack.

5. To complete the design, gently run a quilting tool around the border of each small square to create a stitched effect.

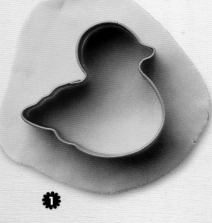

Method

1. Using a non-stick rolling pin, roll out the pink, purple, yellow, and green fondants on a non-stick surface to approximately ⅛ in. (3 mm) in thickness. Use the duck cookie cutter to cut out colored ducks to cover the cookies. Cover any leftover fondant in plastic wrap to stop it from drying out.

2. Apply a thin layer of piping gel to the surface of each cookie, using a fine paintbrush.

3. Carefully lift the fondant ducks with a palette knife and place them on top of the cookies. The piping gel will act as glue and attach the fondant to the cookie.

4. Gently rub a finger around the edge of the fondant to achieve a smooth finish.

5. Allow the fondant to firm for about 30 minutes, and then use edible pens to draw stitching around the edge of each cookie. You can use a similar-colored pen to the fondant (i.e. pink edible pen on the pink duck), or a contrasting color if you desire. Use a black edible pen to draw an eye on each duck.

Bathtime Fun

In this project, you will learn how to add quirky details to cookies using edible pens and fondant decorations.

6. Roll out the red fondant and use a small heart plunger cutter to cut out 1 heart-shaped beak for each duck. Attach the beaks to the cookies using edible glue.

7. Roll out the yellow, pink, purple, and green fondant and use a small flower plunger cutter to cut out a flower for each duck. Attach a flower to the head of each duck using edible glue. To make the center of each flower, press a small ball of fondant into a flower silicone mold. Ensure that the fondant is flush with the back of the mold, and then flex the mold to remove the flower. Attach a molded flower to the center of each flower on the ducks using edible glue. If possible, attach flowers that are different colors to the duck to provide a nice contrast.

8. Use the remaining pink, yellow, green, and purple fondant to make the wings for the ducks using a small leaf cutter. Run a quilting tool down the center of each wing to add a stitched pattern. Attach 1 wing onto each duck using edible glue. If possible, attach a wing that is a different color to the duck and flower.

You will need

Materials: Duck-shaped cookies • Fondant—pink, purple, green, red, yellow • Clear piping gel • Edible pens—pink, black, purple, green, gray • Edible glue
Tools: Non-stick rolling pin • Duck cookie cutter or template (see page 136) • Fine paintbrush • Palette knife • Plunger cutters—small flower and small heart • Small flower silicone mold • Small leaf cutter • Quilting tool

Stamping Style

In this project, you will learn how to use liquid food coloring as edible ink to print pretty motifs onto cookies using rubber stamps.

You will need

Materials: Round cookies • White fondant • Clear piping gel • Black liquid food coloring • Medium-peak white royal icing **Tools:** Non-stick rolling pin • Round cutter (same size as cookies) • Fine paintbrush • Palette knife • Selection of rubber stamps with vintage motifs • Piping bag for the royal icing fitted with a No 2 round decorating tip

Method

1. Using a non-stick rolling pin, roll out the fondant on a non-stick surface to approximately ⅛ in. (3 mm) in thickness. Use the round cutter to cut out circles to cover the cookies.

Tip If you are concerned that the design won't print evenly onto the cookie, press the stamp into the fondant before it is placed on the cookie. If you are happy with the design, you can then use the round cutter to cut around the stamped section and attach it to the top of the cookie.

2. Apply a thin layer of piping gel to the surface of each cookie, using a fine paintbrush. Carefully lift the fondant with a palette knife and place it on top. Gently rub a finger around the edge of the fondant to achieve a smooth finish.

3. Paint black liquid food coloring onto the surface of the rubber stamps, making sure that all of the design is covered. Don't use rubber stamps that have previously been used in non-edible ink. Even if you wash them, there could still be traces of inedible ink on them, which could contaminate your cookies.

4. Press a rubber stamp onto the fondant surface of one cookie, and then carefully remove it to reveal the printed design.

5. Pipe a snail trail around the rim of each cookie, using medium-peak white royal icing in a piping bag fitted with a No 2 round decorating tip (see Technique in Focus, below).

Perfect presentation
Wrap some cookies in a vintage handkerchief and secure it with a lace bow to make a lovely gift.

TECHNIQUE IN FOCUS:
Piping a snail trail
Using a round decorating tip, pipe a dot of medium-peak royal icing of the desired size. Stop squeezing and gently pull the tip through the dot to create a tapered tail. Pipe another tapered dot at the tip of the previous one, ensuring there is no space between the end of one tail and the next dot. Continue to pipe the trail until you reach where you started.

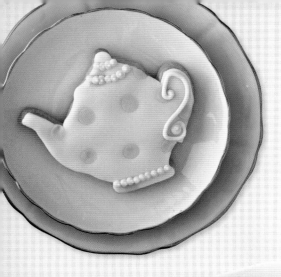

You will need

Materials: Teapot-shaped cookies
• Fondant—pale pink, cerise, pale green
• Clear piping gel • Medium-peak royal
icing—pale green, white, pale pink **Tools:** Non-stick rolling pin • Teapot cookie cutter or template
(see page 137) • Fine paintbrush • Palette knife • No 16
round decorating tip • Scribing tool • Piping bags for the
royal icing, fitted with No 2 round decorating tips

Teapot Delight

In this project, you will learn how to make polka-dot patterns with fondant to decorate fun teapot cookies.

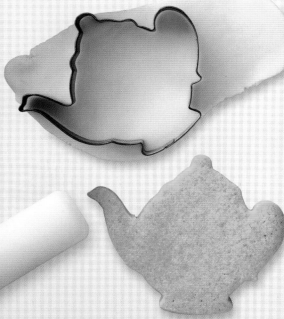

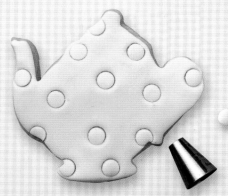

Method

1. Using a non-stick rolling pin, roll out fondant in the color chosen for the teapot on a non-stick surface to approximately ⅛ in. (3 mm) in thickness. Use the teapot cookie cutter to cut out colored teapot shapes to cover the cookies. Apply a thin layer of piping gel to the surface of each teapot cookie, using a fine paintbrush. Using a palette knife, carefully position the fondant teapots on top of the cookies. The piping gel will act as glue and attach the fondant to the cookie.

2. Gently rub a finger around the edge of the fondant to achieve a smooth finish. Press the end of a No 16 round decorating tip into the fondant in a random fashion to create a spotty pattern on the teapot. It is important to do this step while the fondant is still fresh, otherwise it will crack.

3. Use a scribing tool to carefully pick out the spots from the teapot.

TECHNIQUE IN FOCUS:
Piping dots and scrolls

Use a round decorating tip to pipe dots and scrolls. You can use tips with small holes to pipe thin scrolls or small dots. Larger holes produce thicker scrolls and dots.

For the scroll: Touch the decorating tip onto the surface of the cookie. Squeeze the piping bag with a steady pressure until the icing comes out, then carefully lift the tip slightly off the surface of the cookie while still squeezing out the icing. Gently guide the icing into position on the cookie. Once you have finished piping the scroll, stop squeezing the piping bag and gently lower the decorating tip back onto the surface of the cookie to finish.

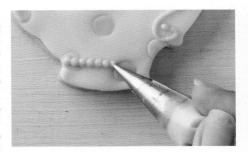

For dots: Squeeze the piping bag with steady pressure. Stop squeezing when the dot is the desired size, then lift the decorating tip away from the cookie. If you have a little peak on top of your dot, gently press it down with a damp paintbrush.

4. Roll out some fondant in the color chosen for the spots and use the No 16 round decorating tip to cut out spots to fill the gaps. Gently stick the spots into the holes using piping gel. Once the spots are in position, gently rub a finger over the surface of the teapot to blend the fondants together.

5. Pipe a scroll handle onto each cookie, using medium-peak royal icing in a piping bag fitted with a No 2 round decorating tip. Pipe small dots around the lid and base of the teapot to complete the design. Leave the cookies to dry for at least four hours before serving.

Add little glittery sugar butterflies to simple round cookies to make elegant bakes for any occasion.

Pastel Butterflies

You will need

Materials: Round cookies (2¼ in. [5.5 cm] in diameter) • Fondant—white, pale green, and pale pink • Clear piping gel • Edible glue • CMC or Tylo powder • Pearl edible glitter • Edible pearls (optional) • Medium-peak pale pink royal icing **Tools:** Non-stick rolling pin • Circle cutter (2¼ in. [5.5 cm] in diameter) • Fine paintbrush • Palette knife • Fluted circle cutter (2 in. [5 cm] in diameter) • Small butterfly plunger cutter • Cardboard or aluminum foil • Piping bag for the royal icing, fitted with a No 1 round decorating tip

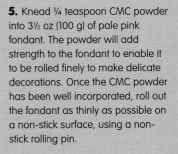

5. Knead ¼ teaspoon CMC powder into 3½ oz (100 g) of pale pink fondant. The powder will add strength to the fondant to enable it to be rolled finely to make delicate decorations. Once the CMC powder has been well incorporated, roll out the fondant as thinly as possible on a non-stick surface, using a non-stick rolling pin.

Method

1. Using a non-stick rolling pin, roll out the pale green fondant on a non-stick surface to approximately ⅛ in. (3 mm) in thickness. Use the circle cookie cutter to cut out rounds to cover each cookie.

2. Apply a thin layer of piping gel to the surface of each cookie, using a fine paintbrush. Carefully lift the fondant rounds with a palette knife and place them on top of the cookies. The piping gel will act as glue and attach the fondant to the cookie.

3. Gently rub a finger around the edge of the fondant to achieve a smooth finish.

4. Roll out the white fondant with a non-stick rolling pin and use the fluted cutter to cut out a fluted circle for each cookie. Use edible glue to attach a fluted circle into the center of each cookie.

Tip To avoid the fluted fondant circles from becoming misshapen when they are attached to the cookies, allow them to dry for a few minutes beforehand.

6. Use a butterfly plunger cutter to cut out a pink butterfly for each cookie. Fold a piece of cardboard or aluminum foil into a V-shape, then place the butterflies into the V and allow them to dry for about an hour until they hold their shape.

7. Once the butterflies are dry, lightly brush them with edible glue and dust them with edible glitter using a paintbrush. Shake off any excess glitter. If desired, attach small edible pearls using royal icing along the spine of each butterfly, to represent the body.

8. Use a small dot of royal icing to attach a butterfly to each cookie, then pipe a little trail of dots of pale pink royal icing leading from the butterfly to the edge of the fluted fondant circle, to represent the flight path of the butterfly.

2

Method

1. Using a non-stick rolling pin, roll out the white fondant on a non-stick surface to approximately ⅛ in. (3 mm) in thickness. Use the circle cookie cutter to cut out fondant rounds.

2. Apply a thin layer of piping gel to the surface of each cookie, using a fine paintbrush. Carefully lift the fondant rounds with a palette knife and place them on top of the cookies. The piping gel will act as glue and attach the fondant to the cookie. Gently rub a finger around the edge of the fondant to achieve a smooth finish.

You will need

Materials: Round cookies (2¼ in. [5.5 cm] in diameter) • White fondant (enough to cover each cookie and make the decorations) • Clear piping gel • Pearl edible luster dust • CMC or Tylo powder • Medium-peak white royal icing • Small white nonpareils (optional) **Tools:** Non-stick rolling pin • Circle cutter (2¼ in. [5.5 cm] in diameter) • Fine paintbrush • Palette knife • Broad soft brush (an unused blusher brush is ideal) • Petunia cutter and silicone veining mold • Embossing mat (lace pattern) • Small leaf cutter • Piping bag for the royal icing, fitted with a No 1 round decorating tip

Flower Fantasy in White

In this project, you will use an embossing mat and a veining mold to create delicate flowers to adorn fondant-topped cookies. Flourishes of royal icing complete the design. The white scheme used in the project can be easily adapted to bolder colors to suit any theme.

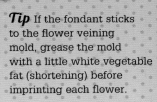

3. If desired, lightly brush pearl edible luster dust over the surface of each cookie using a soft, broad brush.

4. Knead ¼ teaspoon CMC powder into 3½ oz (100 g) of white fondant. The powder will add strength to the fondant, to enable it to be rolled finely to make delicate decorations. Once the CMC powder has been well incorporated, roll out the fondant as thinly as possible on a non-stick board, using a non-stick rolling pin.

5. Use the petunia cutter to cut out 2 flowers for each cookie. Place each flower one at a time into one side of the veining mold. Close the mold over the top of the flower and press firmly to imprint the pattern into both sides of the flower. Open the veining mold, then remove the flower and leave to one side to dry for about 30 minutes until firm.

Tip If the fondant sticks to the flower veining mold, grease the mold with a little white vegetable fat (shortening) before imprinting each flower.

6. Roll out the remaining white fondant and place it over the top of the embossing mat. Firmly roll a rolling pin once over the top of the fondant to imprint the pattern into it. Remove the embossing mat carefully to reveal the design.

7. Use a small leaf cutter to cut out 2 leaves for each cookie from the embossed fondant.

8. Attach flowers and leaves onto the surface of each cookie in a pattern of your choice, using royal icing to secure them in position. Pipe fine vines and dots with white royal icing around the flowers using a No 1 round decorating tip to complete the pattern.

9. If desired, attach small white nonpareils in the center of the flowers, using royal icing to secure them in place.

Baby Shower Favors

In this project, you will learn how to make sweet little umbrella cookies filled with blossoms and a little baby in a bonnet—cute little favors for a baby shower.

You will need

Materials: Umbrella-shaped cookies • Fondant— brown, yellow, pale purple, pale blue, pale pink, pale green, peach • Edible glue • Medium-peak white royal icing • White gum paste • Edible pens—black and red **Tools:** Cake smoother (optional) • Fine paintbrush • Non-stick rolling pin • Umbrella cutter (same size as cookies) or template (see page 137) • Small knife • Cutting wheel • Piping bag for the royal icing, fitted with No 2 round decorating tip • Small round cutter (1 in. [2.5 cm] in diameter) • Veining tool or toothpick • Small leaf plunger cutter • Assorted small blossom cutters • Foam mat • Ball tool

Method

1. Roll a cylinder of brown fondant for the handle of the umbrella. To achieve an even thickness, you can use a cake smoother to roll the fondant if you have one. Attach the handle to the cookie, using edible glue to secure it in place.

5. Use medium-peak white royal icing in a piping bag fitted with a No 2 round decorating tip to pipe two dots of icing at the end of each umbrella. The umbrella is now ready to fill.

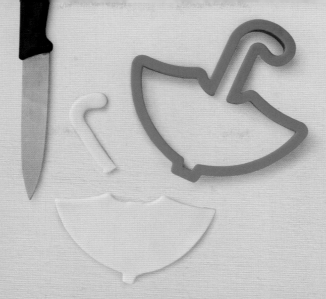

2. Next roll a small cylinder of yellow, purple, or blue fondant and attach it as an arc to the outside edge of the umbrella, using edible glue to secure it in place.

3. Using a non-stick rolling pin on a non-stick surface, roll out the rest of the yellow, purple, and blue fondant to approximately ⅛ in. (3 mm) in thickness. Use the umbrella cutter to cut out an umbrella to cover each cookie. Cut the fondant handle off each umbrella with a small knife, and then attach each one on top of the corresponding-colored fondant arc with edible glue. The arc will lift the fondant umbrella from the cookie so that it can be filled later. It is important to make sure the umbrella is attached so that the fondant arc is not visible.

4. Use a cutting wheel or a small knife to score lines into the umbrella.

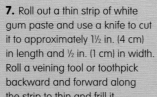

7. Roll out a thin strip of white gum paste and use a knife to cut it to approximately 1½ in. (4 cm) in length and ½ in. (1 cm) in width. Roll a veining tool or toothpick backward and forward along the strip to thin and frill it.

6. To make the baby's head, use a non-stick rolling pin on a non-stick surface to roll out the peach fondant, and use a round cutter to cut out a circle for each cookie.

8. Using edible glue, attach a white strip to the rim of half of the back of each peach circle, pleating it as you go, to make the baby's bonnet.

9. Turn the heads over and use edible pens to draw eyes and lips on each baby.

10. If desired, roll a small curl for the baby's hair using leftover brown fondant, and attach it to the baby's head with edible glue.

Continued next page

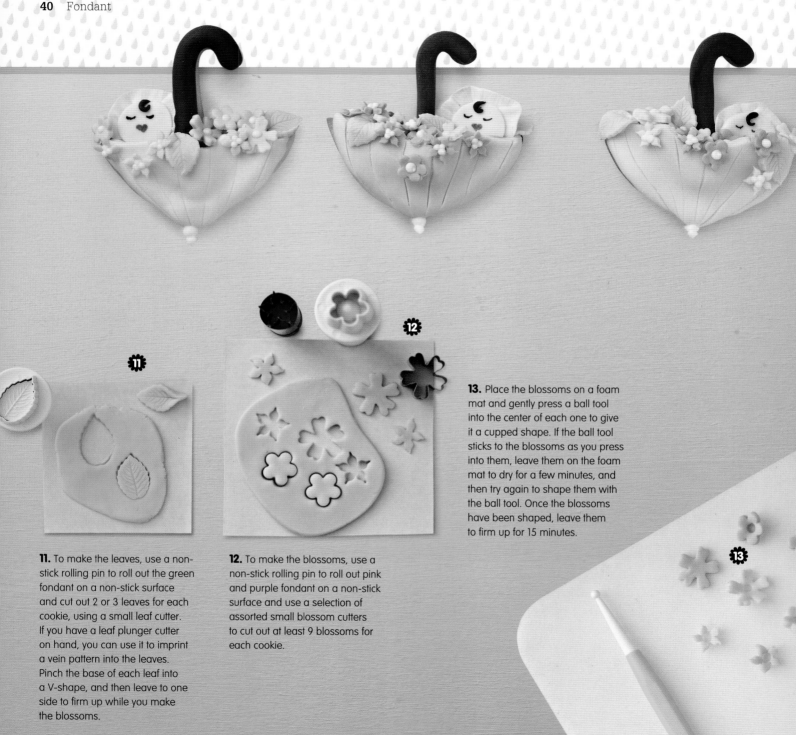

11. To make the leaves, use a non-stick rolling pin to roll out the green fondant on a non-stick surface and cut out 2 or 3 leaves for each cookie, using a small leaf cutter. If you have a leaf plunger cutter on hand, you can use it to imprint a vein pattern into the leaves. Pinch the base of each leaf into a V-shape, and then leave to one side to firm up while you make the blossoms.

12. To make the blossoms, use a non-stick rolling pin to roll out pink and purple fondant on a non-stick surface and use a selection of assorted small blossom cutters to cut out at least 9 blossoms for each cookie.

13. Place the blossoms on a foam mat and gently press a ball tool into the center of each one to give it a cupped shape. If the ball tool sticks to the blossoms as you press into them, leave them on the foam mat to dry for a few minutes, and then try again to shape them with the ball tool. Once the blossoms have been shaped, leave them to firm up for 15 minutes.

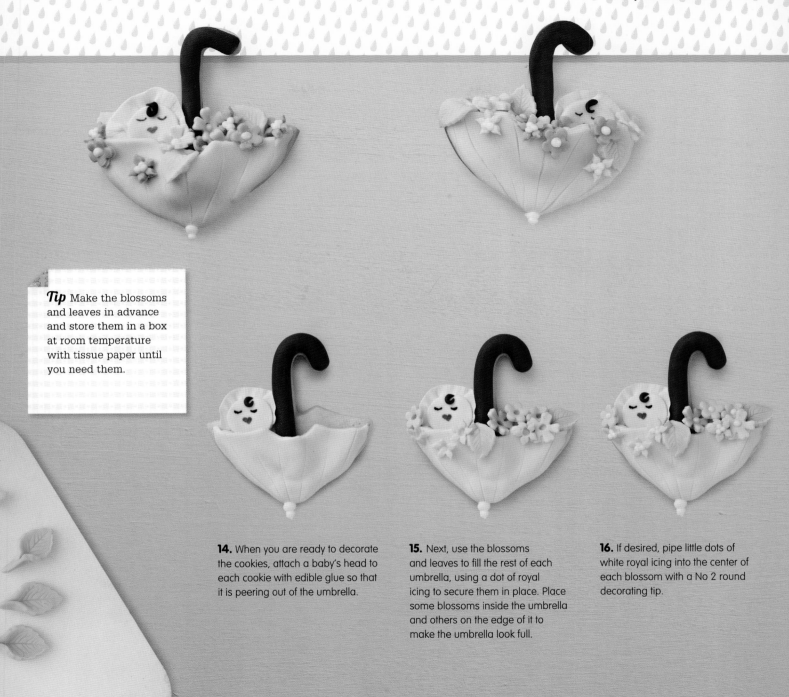

Tip Make the blossoms and leaves in advance and store them in a box at room temperature with tissue paper until you need them.

14. When you are ready to decorate the cookies, attach a baby's head to each cookie with edible glue so that it is peering out of the umbrella.

15. Next, use the blossoms and leaves to fill the rest of each umbrella, using a dot of royal icing to secure them in place. Place some blossoms inside the umbrella and others on the edge of it to make the umbrella look full.

16. If desired, pipe little dots of white royal icing into the center of each blossom with a No 2 round decorating tip.

Six round cookies can be stacked in a pretty pile and decorated with fondant and little handmade strawberries to create miniature tiered celebration cakes—small enough for a doll's house. If you fancy bigger cookie stacks, simply use larger cookies; similarly you can add different decorations to personalize your bake.

Petite Tiered Cookie Cakes

You will need

Materials: Round cookies (2 x 1¾ in. [4.5 cm], 2 x 1½ in. [4 cm], and 2 x 1¼ in. [3 cm] in diameter for each cookie stack) • Medium-peak white royal icing • Fondant—bright pink, green, red • Edible glue **Tools:** Piping bag for the royal icing fitted with a small star decorating tip • Non-stick rolling pin • Cutting wheel or knife • Fine paintbrush • Tiny star cutter • Scribing tool or pin

. . . .

Method

1. Use a small amount of medium-peak white royal icing to stick the cookies of the same size together to make 3 small stacks. If any royal icing oozes out from between the cookie layers, wipe it away with a dry paintbrush.

2. Using a non-stick rolling pin, roll out the bright-pink fondant on a non-stick surface to approximately ⅛ in. (3 mm) in thickness. Place each small stack on top of the fondant, and then use a cutting wheel or small knife to gently cut the fondant out around the cookie in a wiggly pattern.

3. Attach the cut-out fondant to the top and sides of each stack, using edible glue applied with a fine paintbrush to secure it in place. The fondant should look like icing on a cake.

4. Once all 3 stacks have their fondant top added, attach the medium-sized stack to the top of the center of the largest stack, and then the smallest stack to the top of the center of the medium one, using a small amount of royal icing to secure them in position. The cookie stack will look like a miniature 3-tiered cake. It can either be left plain, or you can create some pretty decorations.

5. To make little strawberries for the top of the cookie stack, roll out the green fondant thinly with a non-stick rolling pin on a non-stick surface and use a very small star cutter to cut out a green star for each strawberry. This will represent the hull of the strawberry.

6. Next, roll small balls of red fondant into teardrop shapes no longer than ¼ in. (5 mm). Attach a green star to the top of each strawberry using edible glue. I have made 7 strawberries for each cookie stack, but you can make as many or as few as you wish.

7. Use a scribing tool or fine pin to prick little holes randomly into the surface of each strawberry to represent the seeds.

8. To complete the design, use medium-peak white royal icing in a piping bag fitted with a small star decorating tip to pipe 7 small rosettes (to represent cream) on top of each cookie stack, and then place a strawberry on top of each rosette (with the tip of the strawberry pointing in toward the center of the cookie stack) before it dries.

Ring O' Rose Clusters

In this project, you will learn how to make sweet little roses to decorate your cookies. If you don't have time to make three roses for each cookie, a single rose in the center will look just as pretty.

You will need

Materials: Round fluted-edge cookies (approximately 2 in. [5 cm] in diameter) • White fondant • Clear piping gel • Medium-peak white royal icing • Gum paste—pale pink and pale green **Tools:** Non-stick rolling pin • Fluted circle cutter (2 in. [5 cm] in diameter) • Fine paintbrush • Palette knife • No 3 round decorating tip • Piping bag for the royal icing fitted with No 2 round decorating tip • 1½ in. (4 cm) five-petal rose cutter • Small leaf cutter • Quilting tool • Small knife

Method

1. Using a non-stick rolling pin, roll out the white fondant on a non-stick surface to approximately ⅛ in. (3 mm) in thickness. Use the fluted circle cutter to cut out fluted circles to cover the cookies.

2. Apply a thin layer of piping gel to the surface of each cookie, using a fine paintbrush.

3. Carefully lift the fondant circles off the board with a palette knife and place them on top of the cookies. The piping gel will act as glue and attach the fondant to the cookie.

4. While the fondant is still fresh, press the end of a No 3 round decorating tip around the fluted edge to cut out little holes in the fondant. It is important to do this while the fondant is still fresh, otherwise it will crack.

5. Using a No 2 round decorating tip, pipe white royal icing around the fluted edge of each cookie and allow to dry.

6. To make the roses, roll out the pink gum paste thinly onto a non-stick surface using a non-stick rolling pin and cut out a small flower using the five-petal rose cutter.

7. Roll the first petal (petal 1) into a tight scroll. This will be the center of the rose.

8. Wrap petal 3 around the center petal, making sure it is slightly higher than it. Next, wrap the remaining petals around the center, overlapping them as you go. Start with petal 2.

9. Next, wrap petal 5 and then petal 4 around the center to complete the rose. Use your thumb to gently open out the petals if desired.

10. Trim the base of the rose with a knife so that it can sit upright, and then leave it to one side to dry for about 30 minutes. You will need to make 3 roses to decorate each cookie, but it is always a good idea to make a few extra ones in case you accidentally drop one!

11. To make the leaves, roll out the green gum paste thinly onto a non-stick surface using a non-stick rolling pin and cut out 3 leaves for each cookie using the leaf cutter.

12. Use a quilting tool to gently mark a stitched pattern along the center of each leaf.

13. Pinch the base of each leaf into a V-shape, and then leave to one side to dry for about 30 minutes until firm.

14. When you are ready to decorate the cookies, pipe a small amount of royal icing onto the back of each rose and stick 3 roses clustered together in the center of each cookie. Next, pipe a small amount of royal icing onto the back of each leaf and stick 3 leaves around each rose cluster on each cookie.

Tips

❋ To save time, make the roses and leaves a few days in advance and store them in a box at room temperature once they are dry.

❋ If you find that you have used too much royal icing when attaching the roses and leaves to the cookies and the icing is oozing out from behind the decorations, use a dry paintbrush to gently scrape away the excess royal icing before it sets.

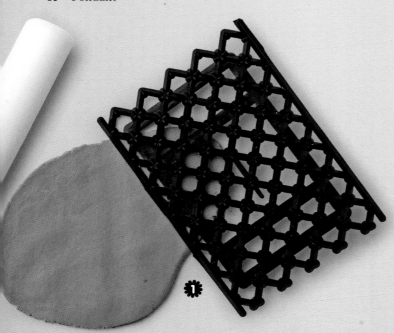

Elegant Embossing

In this project, you will learn how to make ribbon roses to decorate embossed cookies—perfect little treats for a formal occasion or as wedding favors.

You will need

Materials: Square fluted-edge cookies (approximately 2 in. [5 cm] in width) • Fondant— pale gray and white • Clear piping gel • Medium- peak white royal icing • Gum paste—pale gray and white **Tools:** Non-stick rolling pin • Quilting embosser patchwork cutter • Square fluted-edge cutter (2 in. [5 cm] in width) • Fine paintbrush • Palette knife • Piping bag for the royal icing, fitted with a No 1 round decorating tip • Small knife

Method

1. Using a non-stick rolling pin, roll out the white and gray fondant on a non-stick surface to approximately ⅛ in. (3 mm) in thickness. Press a quilting embosser patchwork cutter into the fondant to create a quilted effect. It is important to do this step while the fondant is still fresh, otherwise it will crack.

2. Use the square fluted-edge cutter to cut out fluted squares from the embossed fondant to cover the cookies.

3. Apply a thin layer of clear piping gel to the surface of each cookie, using a fine paintbrush.

4. Carefully lift the fondant squares off the board with a palette knife and place them on top of the cookies. The piping gel will act as glue and attach the fondant to the cookie. Cover half of the cookies with white fondant and the other half with gray fondant.

5. Pipe small dots of medium-peak white royal icing between each diamond on the quilted design, using a No 1 round decorating tip.

Tip Make the ribbon roses in advance so that they have time to dry before adding them to the cookies.

TECHNIQUE IN FOCUS:
Ribbon roses

6. To make the ribbon roses, roll out a strip of gum paste thinly onto a non-stick surface, using a non-stick rolling pin. The longer you roll your strip, the bigger your ribbon rose will be. Aim to make the strip at least 6 in. (15 cm) long and 1¼ in. (3 cm) wide.

7. Starting at one end of the strip, begin to roll it up like a snail shell. This will form the center of your rose.

8. Begin to wrap the strip around the center of the rose, pinching the gum paste into pleats at the base of the rose as you go along to give it a ruffle effect.

9. Once the rose is the size you require, trim off the remaining part of the strip with a small knife.

10. Trim off the tail of the ribbon rose so that the back of the rose is flat.

11. When you are ready to decorate the cookies, pipe a small amount of royal icing onto the back of each rose and stick a white rose onto the top right-hand corner of each gray cookie and a gray rose onto each white cookie.

Tip The thinner you roll out the gum paste for your ribbon roses, the more delicate and frilly they will be.

7

8

9

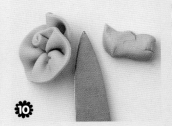

10

48

Colored Dough

Vanilla cookie dough can be colored by gradually kneading in edible food coloring gel until a uniform color is achieved. It is important to use gel colors, because liquid food coloring will make the dough sticky and the cookies will spread during baking. When adding the coloring, bear in mind that cookies will generally bake a little lighter than the dough appears.

Dinky Rabbits & Carrots

In this project, you will learn how to create cute rabbit cookies in a silicone mold, and use thinned colored dough to pipe little carrots.

You will need

Materials: 1 quantity of vanilla cookie dough (see page 131), chilled—colored pink, purple, yellow, lime green (for the rabbits); orange and dark green (for the carrots) • Medium-peak white royal icing **Tools:** Leaping rabbit silicone mold • Small knife • Piping bag for the medium-peak white royal icing, fitted with a No 1 round decorating tip • 2 x piping bags for the cookie dough fitted with No 2 round decorating tips

. . . .

To make the rabbit cookies

Method

1. Press a small ball of pink, purple, yellow, or lime-green colored dough into the rabbit silicone mold so that the dough is flush with the back of the mold. Use a small knife to trim away any excess dough, if necessary.

2. Gently flex the mold to remove the rabbit and place it on a prepared baking sheet. Repeat steps 1 and 2 to create as many rabbits as desired.

3. Bake the rabbits in an oven, following the cookie dough recipe. On average the rabbits will take 6 minutes to bake, as they are relatively small in size.

4. Once cooked, remove the rabbits from the oven and allow them to cool completely on a wire rack before decorating.

5. Pipe a small dot of white royal icing onto the tail of each rabbit to complete the design using a piping bag fitted with a No 1 round decorating tip. Remember to leave the cookies to dry for at least an hour before serving.

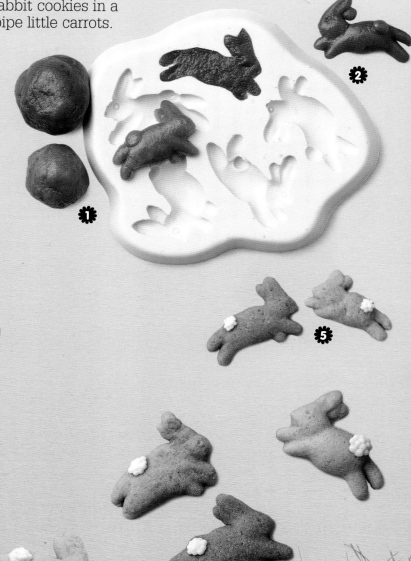

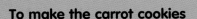

To make the carrot cookies

Method

1. Place the orange and green cookie dough in separate bowls and add approximately 1 tablespoon of cold water to each bowl. Use a spoon to vigorously mix the water into the dough to achieve a smooth consistency, like a soft-serve ice cream. It is important to continue mixing until the dough is smooth and there are no lumps. Add a little more water, 1 teaspoon at a time, if the mixture is too thick.

2. Spoon each dough mixture into a piping bag fitted with a No 2 round decorating tip.

3. Use the orange dough mixture to pipe a zigzag pattern in the shape of a small carrot onto a baking sheet lined with baking parchment. Try to make the carrots no larger than the rabbits.

4. Use the green dough mixture to pipe leaves onto each carrot.

5. Bake the carrots in the oven, following the cookie dough recipe (for approximately 6 minutes) and then allow them to cool completely before serving.

Tip Be careful not to make the thinned dough mixture too runny, otherwise it will dribble out of the piping bag.

On the Ranch

In this project, you will learn how to make two different styles of simple two-tone cookies using vanilla and chocolate cookie dough. The techniques used in this project can be applied to other cookie shapes, so you can easily use different cutters to make the cookies suit a theme of your choice.

Method

To make the cowboy boots and hats

1. Using a non-stick rolling pin, roll out half of the vanilla and chocolate cookie doughs to an even thickness on a non-stick surface. Use the circle cutter to cut out an even number of circles from each dough.

2. Gently press the mini boot and cowboy hat cutters into the center of each circle and carefully remove the shapes.

3. Place the chocolate mini boots and hats into the center of the vanilla circles, and the vanilla mini boots and hats into the center of the chocolate circles. Gently rub a finger over the top of each cookie to blend the 2 cookie doughs together and ensure that the mini shapes are secure inside the circles.

4. Use a palette knife to carefully transfer the cookies onto a prepared baking sheet, and allow the cookies to firm in a freezer for 10 minutes before baking them according to the dough recipe. Once done, remove the cookies from the oven and allow them to cool completely on a wire rack before serving.

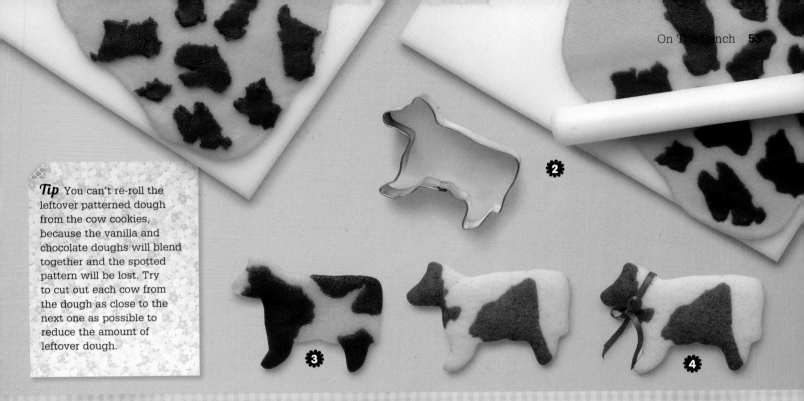

Tip You can't re-roll the leftover patterned dough from the cow cookies, because the vanilla and chocolate doughs will blend together and the spotted pattern will be lost. Try to cut out each cow from the dough as close to the next one as possible to reduce the amount of leftover dough.

You will need

Materials: 1 quantity of vanilla cookie dough (see page 131), chilled • 1 quantity of chocolate cookie dough (see page 130), chilled **Tools:** Non-stick rolling pin • Circle cutter (2⅝ in. (6.5 cm) in diameter) • Mini cowboy hat and cowboy boot cutters (smaller in size than the circle cutter) or templates (see page 136) • Palette knife • Cow cookie cutter or template (see page 136) • Thin red satin ribbon (optional)

Method

To make the Jersey cows

1. Using a non-stick rolling pin, roll out half of the vanilla and chocolate cookie doughs to an even thickness on a non-stick surface.

2. Gently tear the chocolate dough into small, irregular pieces and randomly lay them on the surface of the vanilla dough. Gently roll a non-stick rolling pin over the dough to blend the 2 colors together.

3. Press a cow cookie cutter into the spotted dough to cut out the desired number of cows, and then place them on a prepared baking sheet. Bake the cookies according to the cookie dough recipe, and then allow them to cool completely.

4. If desired, tie a little ribbon bow around the neck of each cow. Remember to remove it before eating, though!

In this project, you will learn how to make a three-dimensional cookie filled with a surprise. Watch your friends' delight as they break open their cookies to find miniature chocolate coins spilling out.

Piggy Banks

You will need

Materials: 1 quantity of vanilla cookie dough (see page 131), chilled and colored pink • Small chocolate beans • Edible gold paint (or edible gold luster dust mixed with water or clear alcohol) • Medium-peak white royal icing • Black edible pen **Tools:** Large non-stick rolling pin • Piggy bank template (see page 136) • Small knife • Small circle cutter (1 in. [2.5 cm] in diameter) • Palette knife • Fine paintbrush • Piping bag for the royal icing, fitted with a No 2 round decorating tip

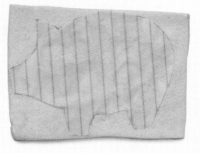

Method

1. Using a non-stick rolling pin, roll out the chilled pink dough on a non-stick surface until it is approximately ¼ in. (5 mm) in thickness. Place the piggy bank template on top of the dough and use it as a guide to cut out 3 piggy bank shapes for each cookie with a small knife.

6. Place a hollowed-out piggy bank cookie on top of the first cookie. If any royal icing oozes out between the 2 cookies, brush it away with a dry paintbrush.

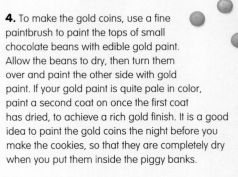

2. Use a small circle cutter or a knife to hollow out the center of a third of the piggy bank shapes. It is important to leave a rim approximately ½ in. (1 cm) wide around the edge of the hollowed-out piggy bank.

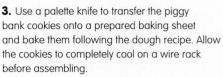

3. Use a palette knife to transfer the piggy bank cookies onto a prepared baking sheet and bake them following the dough recipe. Allow the cookies to completely cool on a wire rack before assembling.

4. To make the gold coins, use a fine paintbrush to paint the tops of small chocolate beans with edible gold paint. Allow the beans to dry, then turn them over and paint the other side with gold paint. If your gold paint is quite pale in color, paint a second coat on once the first coat has dried, to achieve a rich gold finish. It is a good idea to paint the gold coins the night before you make the cookies, so that they are completely dry when you put them inside the piggy banks.

5. To assemble the piggy banks, pipe royal icing around the edge of a solid piggy bank cookie.

7. Pipe royal icing around the edge of the top of the cookie and then fill the hollow cavity (up to the height of the cookie) with gold coins. I managed to get about 25 coins inside my piggy bank, but you can add fewer if you prefer.

8. Place the last solid piggy bank cookie on top and gently press it down to ensure that all layers are joined together.

9. Use a No 2 round decorating tip to pipe a little white tail and a coin slot on each piggy bank. Lastly, add a little eye using a black edible pen. Allow the cookies to dry for about an hour before serving.

2.

4

5

Method

1. Place the colored cookie doughs in separate bowls and add approximately 1 tablespoon of cold water to each bowl. Use a spoon to vigorously mix the water into the dough to achieve a smooth consistency. It is important to continue mixing until the mixture is smooth and there are no lumps. Add a little more water, 1 teaspoon at a time, if the mixture is too thick.

2. Spoon each dough mixture into a piping bag fitted with a No 2 round decorating tip.

Tips

✿ Bear in mind that colors are likely to lighten during baking.

✿ Try making different patterns by piping vertical lines of dough before adding the marbled effect.

You will need

Materials: 1 quantity of vanilla cookie dough (see page 131), chilled—colored blue, yellow, green • Edible pen **Tools:** Square cookie cutter (2½ in. [6.5 cm] in width) • Scribing tool • 4 x piping bags for the cookie dough, fitted with No 2 round decorating tips

. . . .

6

3. Line a baking sheet with parchment paper. Using the square cutter as a template, draw evenly spaced squares on the parchment paper with an edible pen.

4. Next, pipe evenly spaced lines of yellow dough diagonally across each square. It is best to pipe slightly over the edge of the square template. It doesn't matter if the edges are uneven, since they will be reshaped later.

5. Pipe lines of blue dough next to each yellow line. Complete the pattern by piping lines of red dough, then lines of green dough until the entire square outline is filled. There should be no gaps between the piped lines.

6. Drag the scribing tool through the colored dough in evenly spaced vertical straight lines to create a marbled effect. Next, drag the scribing tool through the colored dough in evenly spaced horizontal straight lines to complete the pattern.

Kaleidoscope Cookies

In this project, you will learn how to make psychedelic cookies, by piping thinned colored dough and using a scribing tool to create a marbled pattern.

7

7. Bake the squares in the oven, following the dough recipe. While they are still warm, press the square cutter over the top of each cookie to cut off the jagged edges. Allow the cookies to cool completely before serving.

Edible Icing Sheets

Using edible icing sheets is an easy way to instantly add patterns and decorations to your cookies. There are many patterns available to buy, or you can print your own. The sheets can be printed with a normal printer, but the printer must be new and only used for food purposes. Edible ink cartridges and sheets of edible icing paper are available from cake decorating supply stores.

Jigsaw Fun

Use images printed on edible icing sheets to make fun jigsaw cookies—perfect little treats for kids or as a gift for someone special. In this project we have used a gorgeous vintage design from a stationery designer (www.hiphiphooray.com), but there are many other patterned edible sheets to choose from in cake-decorating supply stores. Alternatively, you can send images that you would like to have printed to cake shops to print for you, or print them yourself if you have your own printer jwith edible ink.

You will need

Materials: Jigsaw cookies • White fondant • Clear piping gel • Edible icing sheets printed with images approximately the same size as the cookies • Edible glue

Tools: Rectangular four-piece jigsaw cutter or template (see page 137) • Non-stick rolling pin • Fine paintbrush • Palette knife • Scribing tool or pin • Scissors

Presentation idea

Fold an envelope from colored paper or card stock to put jigsaws into.

5. Place the jigsaw cookie cutter over the top of the edible image and gently mark the outline of each jigsaw piece with a scribing tool or pin.

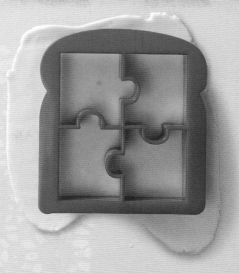

Method

1. To make the jigsaw cookies, cut out the cookie dough using a rectangular four-piece jigsaw cutter or template. Do not separate the jigsaw pieces before baking. Immediately after the cookies are removed from the oven, use the jigsaw cutter to recut the jigsaw into separate pieces again, then allow them to cool completely before decorating.

2. Using a non-stick rolling pin, roll out the white fondant on a non-stick surface to approximately ⅛ in. (3 mm) in thickness. Use the jigsaw cutter to cut out the jigsaw pieces from the fondant to cover the cookies.

3. Apply a thin layer of piping gel to the surface of each cookie, using a fine paintbrush.

4. Carefully lift the fondant jigsaw pieces with a palette knife and place them on top of the corresponding cookies. The piping gel will act as glue and attach the fondant to the cookie.

6. Remove the jigsaw cutter, and then cut out each jigsaw piece from the edible image carefully with scissors.

7. Attach the edible image to the fondant-covered jigsaw pieces, using edible glue to secure it in place.

In this project, you will learn how to use edible icing sheets to decorate pretty party dresses. There are many patterned edible icing sheets available, or you can use plain-colored sheets and then add further decorations to make the cookies more ornate if desired.

Party Dresses

You will need

Materials: Dress cookies • White fondant • Clear piping gel • Edible icing sheets printed with a pattern of your choice • White gum paste • Edible glue • Medium-peak white royal icing (optional) **Tools:** Non-stick rolling pin • Dress cutter or template (see page 137) • Fine paintbrush • Palette knife • Small knife • Silicone bow mold • Piping bag for the royal icing, fitted with a No 1 round decorating tip (optional)

Method

1. Using a non-stick rolling pin, roll out the white fondant on a non-stick surface to approximately ⅛ in. (3 mm) in thickness. Use the dress cutter to cut out the fondant to cover the cookies.

2. Apply a thin layer of piping gel to the surface of each cookie, using a fine paintbrush.

3. Carefully lift the fondant dresses with a palette knife and place them on top of the cookies. The piping gel will act as glue and attach the fondant to the cookie.

4. Use the dress cutter to cut out dresses from the edible icing sheet.

7. To make a bow, press a small ball of white gum paste into a bow silicone mold so that the gum paste is flush with the back of the mold. Use a knife to trim off any excess gum paste if necessary. Flex the mold to carefully remove the bow, before attaching it to the center of the sash with edible glue or a dot of royal icing.

8. If desired, pipe a string of dots of white royal icing into the neckline of each dress to make necklaces.

5. Attach the edible icing dresses to the fondant-covered cookies, using a small amount of edible glue to secure it in place.

6. To add a sash to the waist of each dress, roll out a thin strip of white gum paste and use a knife to cut it to the width of the waist of the dress. Attach it to the dress with edible glue.

Vintage Floral Union Jacks

Use floral and polka-dot edible icing sheets to make stylized flag cookies—perfect little treats for a tea party. In this project, I have used a Union Jack flag template, but any template can be used, along with any type of patterned edible icing sheet to suit any theme.

You will need

Materials: Rectangular cookies • White fondant • Clear piping gel • Patterned edible icing sheets • Edible glue **Tools:** Non-stick rolling pin • Rectangular cutter • Fine paintbrush • Palette knife • Scissors • Union Jack template • Scribing tool or pin

Template

Method

1. Using a non-stick rolling pin, roll out the white fondant on a non-stick surface to approximately ⅛ in. (3 mm) in thickness. Use the rectangular cutter to cut out the fondant to cover the cookies.

2. Apply a thin layer of piping gel to the surface of each cookie, using a fine paintbrush.

3. Carefully lift the fondant rectangular pieces with a palette knife and place them on top of the cookies.

4. Print the Union Jack template at the same size as your rectangular cookie cutter. Using a pair of scissors, cut out the dark sections of the template. Place each section on an edible icing sheet and gently mark the outline with a scribing tool or pin. I have used a blue polka-dot icing sheet for the central and diagonal crosses and a floral icing sheet for the triangular sections.

5. Cut out each edible icing sheet section with scissors.

6. Reassemble the edible icing sheet sections back into the Union Jack configuration and attach them to the fondant-covered cookies, using edible glue to secure them in place. Use the Union Jack template as a reference to ensure that each section is positioned correctly.

Gingham Owls

In this project, you will use edible icing sheets to add fun gingham accents to cute little owls.

①

Method

1. Using a non-stick rolling pin, roll out the pink, blue, and green fondant on a non-stick surface to approximately ⅛ in. (3 mm) in thickness. Use the owl cutter to cut out the fondant to cover the cookies.

Tip If you don't have small round cutters, the bottom (larger end) or tip of round decorating tips can be used instead!

You will need

Materials: Owl cookies • Fondant—pink, blue, green, black, white, orange • Clear piping gel • Edible icing sheets printed with gingham pattern • Edible glue **Tools:** Non-stick rolling pin • Owl cookie cutter or template (see page 138) • Fine paintbrush • Palette knife • Circle cutters (½ in. (1.5 cm), ¾ in. (2 cm), and 1½ in. (4 cm) in diameter) • No 3 and No 18 round decorating tips • Small knife

6. Roll out the remaining pink, blue, and green fondant and use the ¾ in. (2 cm) circle cutter to cut out 2 circles for each owl with a gingham head. For the owls with a fondant head, use the same cutter to cut out two gingham circles from the icing sheets. Use edible glue to attach the circles to each owl.

7. Roll out the white fondant and use the ½ in. (1.5 cm) circle cutter to cut out 2 white circles for each owl. Attach the circles to the colored circles, using edible glue to secure them in place.

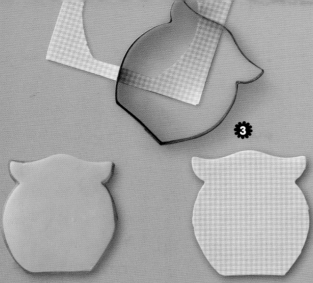

2. Apply a thin layer of piping gel to the surface of each cookie, using a fine paintbrush. Carefully lift the fondant owls with a palette knife and place them on top of the cookies. The piping gel will act as glue and attach the fondant to the cookie.

3. Use the owl cutter to cut out a gingham silhouette from the edible icing sheets for each cookie.

4. Place the 1½ in. (4 cm) circle cutter over the bottom half of each gingham owl and press it down firmly to cut out a semicircle. Attach 1 semicircle, using edible glue, to each chest of half of the fondant-covered owl cookies.

5. Attach the remaining gingham cut-outs to the other half of the fondant-covered owl cookies, using edible glue. Half of the owls will have a gingham chest, and the other half will have a gingham head (see finished owls, opposite).

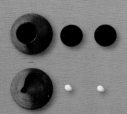

8. Roll out the black fondant and use the end of a No 18 round decorating tip to cut out 2 black circles for each owl. Attach the circles to the white circles, using edible glue to secure them in place.

9. Roll out the remaining white fondant and use the tip of a No 3 round decorating tip to cut out 2 small circles for each owl. Attach the circles to the black circles, using edible glue.

10. To make the beak, roll out the orange fondant and cut out a small triangle for each owl, using a knife. Attach the triangle (tip pointing down) to the center of each owl's head, using edible glue.

11. Use the remaining orange fondant to roll 6 small balls for each owl and attach 3 as the left foot and 3 as the right foot on the bottom of each owl, using edible glue to secure them in place.

Royal Icing

Royal icing can be prepared to different consistencies, making it an extremely useful medium for covering cookies, assembling three-dimensional cookie structures, and piping intricate designs and decorations. Any leftover icing should be emptied out of piping bags and into a bowl, tightly covered with plastic wrap, and then stored in the refrigerator. Stir well before using it again.

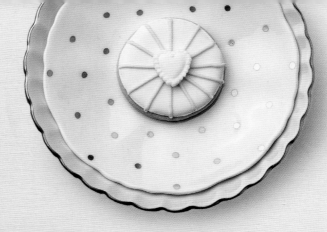

Pretty Pinstripes

These fun little cookies will help you master piping straight lines in no time at all. While this project features little molded hearts in the center of each cookie, different molds can be used to suit any theme.

Tip Freshly made royal icing is always preferable to use over older icing for piping, since it holds its shape and is stiffer and therefore easier to control.

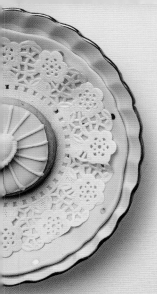

Method

1. Pipe an outline on each round cookie using medium-peak pale blue, white, or pink royal icing in a piping bag fitted with a No 2 round decorating tip.

2. Flood the surface of each cookie with the same-colored thinned royal icing in the squeeze bottle by applying it inside the outlined section. Be careful not to overfill the cookie, otherwise the royal icing will leak over the edge. Leave the cookies to dry for at least 6 hours.

3. Once dry, begin in the center of the cookie and pipe lines of medium-peak royal icing radiating out to the edge of the cookie, using a No 2 round decorating tip. It is best to use a different color of royal icing for the lines to that of the icing on the

surface of the cookie. To ensure that the lines are evenly spaced, it is easiest to pipe four lines to divide the cookie into quarters first and then pipe additional lines to complete the design.

4. Make a small heart for each cookie by pressing a ball of gum paste into a heart silicone mold so that the gum paste is flush with the back of the mold. Use a small knife to trim off any excess gum paste if necessary, then flex the mold to carefully remove the heart.

5. Pipe small dots of medium-peak white royal icing around the edge of each heart, using a No 1 round decorating tip. Allow the dots to dry before attaching each heart to the center of a cookie with a small dot of royal icing.

TECHNIQUE IN FOCUS:
Piping straight lines

❂ Hold the piping bag fitted with a round decorating tip in your right hand (if you are right handed) and use your left hand to hold the bag steady. Don't start squeezing the icing out of the bag until the decorating tip is in contact with the surface of the cookie.

❂ As the icing starts to come out of the decorating tip, lift the tip from the surface of the cookie, while still squeezing the piping bag.

❂ When the icing is the length you need, stop squeezing the bag and place the icing strand down on the surface of the cookie by lowering the decorating tip to the point on the cookie where you would like the straight line to finish.

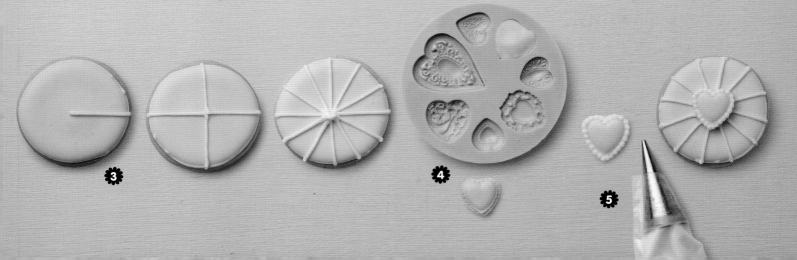

Heart Cookie Pops

By simply inserting a cookie stick into dough before baking, your cookies will be transformed into "cookie pops." In this project, you will make adorable little heart cookie pops decorated with royal icing and handmade bows. These sweet treats could be clustered together as a bouquet to give to someone special, or displayed on a stand as part of a dessert table.

Baking the cookies on a stick

Method

1. Roll out chilled cookie dough with a large non-stick rolling pin, using spacers to ensure that it is an even thickness.

2. Cut out hearts of dough using a heart cutter and then gently insert a cookie stick into the base of each cookie. If the cookie stick pokes out of the back of the cookie, patch up the break with spare cookie dough.

3. Carefully pinch the bottom of the cookie to ensure that it is secure on the cookie stick, and then place it on a prepared baking sheet.

4. Bake the cookies following the dough recipe, and then allow them to cool completely before decorating.

You will need

Materials: Cookie dough (chilled) • White gum paste • Edible glue • Medium-peak royal icing—pink, white • Thinned pink royal icing in a squeeze bottle **Tools:** Large and small non-stick rolling pins • Spacers • Small heart cookie cutter • Cookie sticks • Small knife • Fine paintbrush • Piping bags fitted with No 2 and No 1 round decorating tips • Pin or toothpick • Ribbon (optional)

Continued next page

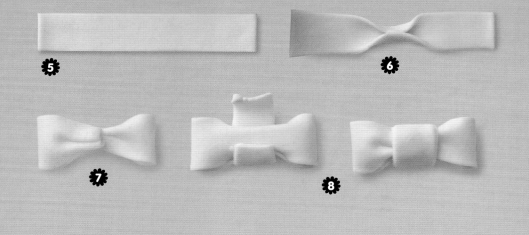

Making the bows

5. Knead the white gum paste until it is soft and pliable. Using a small non-stick rolling pin, roll out the gum paste on a non-stick surface and trim it with a small knife into a strip approximately ½ in. (1.5 cm) wide and 2 in. (5 cm) long.

6. Pinch the center of the strip together with your fingers and apply edible glue to the top of the pinched section with a fine paintbrush.

7. Fold each end of the strip, one at a time, in toward the center, securing them down on top of the edible glue.

8. Cut out a thin strip of white gum paste approximately ½ in. (1.5 cm) wide and 1 in. (2.5 cm) long. Apply edible glue to the back of the strip and then place the center of the strip (glue side down) over the top of the center of the bow and secure the ends of the strip on the underside of the bow. Leave the bow to dry while preparing the cookies.

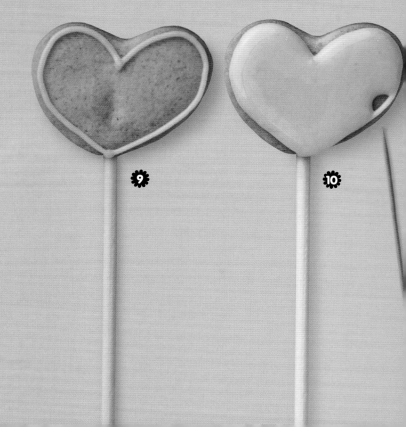

Decorating the cookies with royal icing

9. Pipe the outline of each cookie, using medium-peak pink royal icing in a piping bag fitted with a No 2 round decorating tip.

10. Apply the thinned pink royal icing in the squeeze bottle into the outlined section on each cookie to flood it with royal icing. Be careful not to overfill the cookie, otherwise the royal icing will leak over the edge of the outline. Sometimes air bubbles may appear in the royal icing, so have a pin or toothpick on hand to pop them!

11. Pipe small dots around the pink outline of the cookie if desired, using medium-peak white royal icing in a piping bag fitted with a No 1 round decorating tip.

12. Leave the cookies to dry for at least 6 hours (preferably overnight) before attaching the bows to them with a small amount of royal icing.

13. Once the cookies have dried, tie a small bow with thin ribbon at the top of each cookie stick, if desired.

In this project, you will learn how to create pretty striped and polka-dot gifts using royal icing. Although gift-shaped cookie cutters are available, you can create your own gift cookies using square and heart cutters instead!

Gorgeous Gifts

You will need

Materials: Cookie dough (chilled) • Medium-peak royal icing—turquoise, lilac, white • Thinned lilac, white, and turquoise royal icing in squeeze bottles • White gum paste • Edible silver paint (or edible silver luster dust mixed with water or clear alcohol) **Tools:** Non-stick rolling pin • Square cutter (2¼ in. [6 cm] in width) • Heart cutter (1¾ in. [4.5 cm] in width at widest point) • Small knife • Palette knife • 3 x piping bags for the turquoise, lilac, and white royal icing, fitted with No 2 round decorating tips • Piping bag for the white royal icing, fitted with a No 1 round decorating tip (optional) • Fine paintbrush • Brooch silicone mold

6. While the icing is still wet, use the thinned white royal icing in the squeeze bottle to pipe polka dots into the lilac icing. For the turquoise boxes, use the same royal icing to pipe thin white vertical stripes in the turquoise icing (see finished gifts, above). The white dots and stripes will sink into the lilac and turquoise icing.

7. Flood the outlined lids of all of the cookies with the thinned white royal icing in the squeeze bottle.

8. Leave the cookies to dry for at least 6 hours (preferably overnight).

Method

Preparing the cookies to bake

1. Roll out the chilled cookie dough with a non-stick rolling pin on a non-stick surface to approximately ¼ in. (5 mm) in thickness. Cut out a square and a heart shape to make each gift, using the cutters.

2. Use a knife to cut the tip off each heart, and then attach them to the top of each square using milk or water to secure them in place. Your gift shape is now complete. Use a palette knife to gently lift the gifts onto a lined baking sheet.

3. Bake the cookies according to the dough recipe and then allow them to cool completely before decorating.

Decorating the cookies with royal icing

4. Pipe an outline of a box on each cookie, using medium-peak lilac or turquoise royal icing in a piping bag fitted with a No 2 round decorating tip. Use medium-peak white royal icing in a piping bag fitted with a No 2 round decorating tip to pipe an outline of a lid on top of each box.

5. Flood the inside of the outlined area of each box, using thinned icing from the squeeze bottles in the same color as the outline (either lilac or turquoise). Be careful not to overfill the cookie, otherwise the royal icing will leak over the edge of the outline.

9. Once the cookies are dry, pipe a lilac or turquoise ribbon on top of each gift, using medium-peak royal icing in piping bags fitted with No 2 round decorating tips.

10. If desired, use medium-peak white royal icing in a piping bag fitted with a No 1 round decorating tip to pipe a delicate pattern, such as little dots or lacy loops, underneath each lid to hide the gap between the box and the lid.

11. While the cookies are drying, roll a small ball of white gum paste and press it into a brooch silicone mold, to make a small brooch for each cookie. Flex the mold to remove the brooches, and allow them to firm up before painting them with edible silver paint, using a fine paintbrush. Leave the brooches to one side to dry for a few minutes.

12. Attach a brooch at the base of each bow with a small dot of royal icing.

In this project, you will learn how to create a quilted effect with royal icing to make elegant cookies adorned with handmade frilly flowers.

Quilted Cookies

You will need

Materials: Square cookies (approximately 2½ in. [6 cm] in width) • Medium-peak royal icing—eucalyptus green and white • Thinned royal icing in a squeeze bottle—eucalyptus green • White gum paste • Edible glue • Edible pearls (optional)
Tools: Piping bag for the medium-peak royal icing, fitted with No 2 round decorating tip • Non-stick rolling pin • Small five-petal rose cutter • Foam mat • Bone tool • Paint palette • Fine paintbrush

Method

Decorating the cookies

1. Pipe the outline of each square cookie, using medium-peak eucalyptus green royal icing in a piping bag fitted with a No 2 round decorating tip. Be sure to leave space around the edge of the cookie to allow a border to be piped at the end.

2. Pipe a diagonal line across the cookie (from one corner to the opposite corner), then pipe a second diagonal line, joining the other 2 corners, to create a cross in the center of the cookie. Pipe evenly spaced diagonal lines on either side of the cross to create a diamond pattern on the cookie.

Tip If you are worried about the diamonds leaking into each other, you can use a No 3 round decorating tip to create the outlines on the cookie. This decorating tip will create thicker lines and make a higher barrier between each diamond.

3. Use a squeeze bottle to carefully fill every second diamond with thinned eucalyptus green icing. Be careful not to overfill each diamond, otherwise the royal icing will leak over the edge of the cookie or into an unfilled diamond.

4. Allow the icing to harden for at least 4 hours before filling the remaining diamonds with thinned eucalyptus green royal icing.

5. Allow the cookies to dry completely and then pipe a small dot at the point of each diamond, using medium-peak white royal icing in a piping bag fitted with a No 2 round decorating tip.

6. If desired, pipe a snail trail along the edge of each cookie using medium-peak white royal icing in a piping bag fitted with a No 2 round decorating tip (see page 31).

Making the flowers

7. Knead the white gum paste until it is soft and pliable. Using a small non-stick rolling pin, roll out the gum paste thinly on a non-stick surface. Use the 5-petal rose cutter to cut out 3 small flowers and place them on a foam mat.

8. Use a bone tool to gently thin and ruffle the edges of each petal of the flowers.

9. Gently place 1 flower into the well of a paint palette and arrange the petals so that they overlap and are in the position in which you would like them to dry.

10. Using a fine paintbrush, add a little bit of edible glue to the center of the flower in the well and then place another flower on top of it, again arranging the petals so that they overlap.

11. Add more edible glue to the center of the flower and place the last flower on top. If desired, add edible pearls or dragées to the center of the flower, using edible glue to secure them in place. Repeat this process to make a flower for each cookie.

12. Allow the flowers to dry overnight before attaching each one to the top corner of a cookie with a small amount of royal icing.

In this project, you will assemble gorgeous little three-dimensional gingerbread birdhouses and then decorate them with royal icing and fondant. And what birdhouse would be complete without sweet little bluebirds? This delightful little birdhouse will make a gorgeous table centerpiece for a special celebration and will wow your family and friends… ssshhh—don't let them know that it was easier to make than it looks!

Birdhouse Beauties

You will need

Materials: Fondant—pale blue, red • Paisley-shaped vanilla cookies • Edible glue • Medium-peak white royal icing • Black edible pen • Gingerbread dough (chilled)

Tools: Non-stick rolling pins—large and small • Small paisley-shaped cutter (same size as paisley cookies) or template (see page 138) • Fine paintbrush • Piping bag for the royal icing, fitted with a No 2 round decorating tip • Birdhouse template (see page 138) • Small knife • Circle cutter (¾ in. [2 cm] in diameter) • Palette knife • Piping bag for the royal icing, fitted with a No 16 round decorating tip

. . . .

Method

1 **2** **3** **4**

To make the bluebirds

1. Use a small non-stick rolling pin to roll out the pale-blue fondant on a non-stick surface until it is approximately ⅛ in. (3 mm) in thickness. Cut out one paisley shape for each bird using the paisley cutter and then attach the fondant to the paisley cookies, using a fine paintbrush and edible glue.

2. Pipe a wing onto each bird, using medium-peak white royal icing in a piping bag fitted with a No 2 round decorating tip. A wing can easily be created by piping three teardrops in a fan shape, with their tips touching.

3. Add a beak by shaping a small ball of red fondant into a triangle and then attach it to the side of the head of the bird with a little bit of edible glue.

4. Lastly, use a black edible pen to draw an eye for each bird. Allow the cookies to dry for approximately 1 hour.

5

To make the birdhouse

5. Use a large non-stick rolling pin to roll out the chilled gingerbread dough on a lightly floured surface until it is approximately ¼ in. (5 mm) in thickness. Place the three sections of the birdhouse template on top of the dough and use a knife to carefully cut around the template. You will need to cut out 3 squares, 2 rectangles, and 2 pentagons for each birdhouse. Use a small circle cutter to cut out a hole in one of the pentagons—this will be the entrance to the birdhouse. Use a palette knife to lift the cookies onto a lined baking sheet, and then bake according to the dough recipe. Allow the cookies to cool completely before assembling.

Tip When assembling the birdhouse, you may need to hold each gingerbread piece in position for a few minutes until the royal icing starts to set, before adding the next piece.

Continued next page

6. Place one of the square cookies face up on a board. This will be the base of the birdhouse. Use a generous amount of royal icing to attach one pentagon cookie (without the hole) perpendicularly on top of the square, approximately ½ in. (1.5 cm) from the left-hand edge of the cookie. Make sure that the smooth side (top) of the pentagon cookie is facing outward.

7. Next, use royal icing to attach the long side of one rectangular cookie to the side of the pentagon cookie. The short side of the rectangle should touch the base of the birdhouse, and can be secured in position with extra royal icing. Again, make sure that the smooth side of the rectangular cookie is facing outward.

8. Attach the other pentagon cookie (with the hole cut out) to the other long side of the rectangular cookie with royal icing, so that it is parallel to the first pentagon cookie. The smooth side of the pentagon cookie should be facing outward. There should also be up to 1 in. (2.5 cm) between the pentagon cookie and the right-hand edge of the base cookie.

12. Roll out the red fondant until it is approximately ⅛ in. (3 mm) in thickness. Use the circle cutter to cut out rounds of fondant. You will need up to 35 fondant circles for each birdhouse. Use a small knife to cut each circle in half, and then attach the semicircles in rows on the roof, using edible glue to secure them in place.

13. Start at the bottom of the roof and then gradually build up the layers of semicircles, overlapping with the previous row until you reach the top. Continue to add semicircles until both sides of the roof are covered. If the edges of some semicircles overlap the edge of the roof, trim them with a knife.

14. Pipe a thick snail trail of white royal icing along the ridge and edges of the roof, using a No 16 round decorating tip.

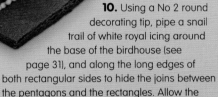

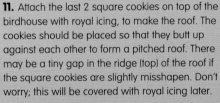

9. Attach the last rectangular cookie in between the two pentagon cookies with royal icing, to complete the sides of the birdhouse. If you can see a lot of royal icing oozing outside the birdhouse onto the base, use a dry paintbrush to scrape it away before it completely dries.

10. Using a No 2 round decorating tip, pipe a snail trail of white royal icing around the base of the birdhouse (see page 31), and along the long edges of both rectangular sides to hide the joins between the pentagons and the rectangles. Allow the birdhouse to dry for about 15 minutes before adding the roof.

11. Attach the last 2 square cookies on top of the birdhouse with royal icing, to make the roof. The cookies should be placed so that they butt up against each other to form a pitched roof. There may be a tiny gap in the ridge (top) of the roof if the square cookies are slightly misshapen. Don't worry; this will be covered with royal icing later.

15. If desired, pipe small dots of white royal icing around the edge of the hole in the front of the birdhouse, using a No 2 round decorating tip.

16. To complete the birdhouse, pipe a snail trail border around the edge of the square base, using white royal icing in a piping bag fitted with a No 2 round decorating tip.

17. Use royal icing to attach some of the bluebirds on the birdhouse, if desired.

Method

1. Use thinned royal icing in a squeeze bottle to pipe small domes approximately ½ in. (1 cm) in diameter onto waxed paper. While the icing is still wet, sprinkle the domes with the pearl nonpareils. Allow the domes to dry (preferably overnight).

2. Using a non-stick rolling pin, roll out the pink fondant on a non-stick surface to approximately ⅛ in. (3 mm) in thickness. Use the circle cutter to cut out rounds from the fondant to cover the cookies.

3. Apply a thin layer of clear piping gel to the surface of each cookie, using a fine paintbrush.

4. Carefully lift the fondant rounds with a palette knife and place them on top of the cookies. The piping gel will act as glue and attach the fondant to the cookie.

In this project, you will use the brush embroidery technique to create a delicate lace effect. This technique is quite easy to master, but it is time consuming—so if time is limited, you can modify the design to feature smaller roses.

Feathered Wild Roses

You will need

Materials: Thinned white royal icing in a squeeze bottle • Pearl nonpareils • Fondant—pale pink • Round cookies (approximately 2¾ in. [7 cm] in diameter) • Clear piping gel • Medium-peak white royal icing **Tools:** Waxed paper • Non-stick rolling pin • Circle cutter (approximately 2¾ in. [7 cm] in diameter) • Fine paintbrush • Paper towel • Palette knife • 5-petal rose cutters (2½ in. [6.5 cm] and 1¾ in. [4.5 cm] in diameter) • Piping bag for the medium-peak royal icing, fitted with a No 2 round decorating tip

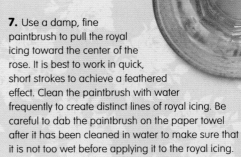

5. Center the large 5-petal rose cutter over the top of each cookie and press it lightly into the fondant. You will need to do this before the fondant has dried, otherwise it will crack. After removing the cutter, you will see an embossed pattern of the rose, which will act as a template for your brush embroidery design. Press the smaller rose cutter into the center of the larger embossed rose to create an imprint for the center of the rose.

6. Pipe medium-peak white royal icing around the outside edge of the rose using a No 2 round decorating tip. It is best to pipe only a small section at first, to prevent the royal icing from drying before you have time to paint it.

7. Use a damp, fine paintbrush to pull the royal icing toward the center of the rose. It is best to work in quick, short strokes to achieve a feathered effect. Clean the paintbrush with water frequently to create distinct lines of royal icing. Be careful to dab the paintbrush on the paper towel after it has been cleaned in water to make sure that it is not too wet before applying it to the royal icing.

8. Repeat the technique for the inner section of the rose until the design is complete.

9. Attach a dry pearl dome into the center of each rose, using a dot of royal icing to secure it in place.

10. Pipe a snail trail around the rim of the cookie (see page 31) using the medium-peak white royal icing in the piping bag. Allow the cookies to dry for 4 hours before serving.

Spring Bouquets

In this project, you will learn how to pipe a bouquet of spring flowers in royal icing, using round decorating tips. These cookies would be perfect little treats for Mother's Day.

You will need

Materials: Cookie dough (chilled) • Medium-peak royal icing—green, purple, white, yellow, pink **Tools:** Non-stick rolling pin • Bouquet-shaped template (see page 139) • Small knife • Palette knife • Piping bag for the green royal icing, fitted with a No 2 round decorating tip • Piping bags for the purple, white, yellow, and pink royal icing, fitted with No 1 round decorating tips • Thin satin ribbon (optional)

Method

1. Roll out the chilled cookie dough on a lightly floured surface to approximately ¼ in. (5 mm) in thickness, using a non-stick rolling pin. Place the bouquet template on top of the dough and use a knife to carefully cut around the template. Use a palette knife to lift the bouquet cookies onto a lined baking sheet, and then bake following the dough recipe. Allow the cookies to cool completely before decorating.

2. Pipe the stems of the flowers onto each cookie, using medium-peak green royal icing in a piping bag fitted with a No 2 round decorating tip. Allow the stems to dry and then pipe more stems on top, to add depth to the bouquet.

3. Use the pink royal icing in a piping bag fitted with a No 1 round decorating tip to pipe little rosebuds onto some of the stems. To create the rose shape, simply pipe a small round spiral, starting from the outside and finishing in the center.

4. To add lavender to the bouquet, use the purple royal icing in a piping bag fitted with a No 1 round decorating tip to pipe small purple dots on either side of the top third of a stem. You can also pipe white dots of royal icing on either side of the top third of some of the stems to create white lavender.

5. To create small daisies, pipe four dots of white royal icing in a blossom shape, using a No 1 round decorating tip, then pipe a small dot of yellow royal icing in the center of the daisy.

6. Allow the cookies to dry for approximately 4 hours. If desired, tie a thin satin ribbon into a bow around the base of the stems of each bouquet before serving. Remember to remove the ribbon before eating!

Teddy Bears

There are many different decorating tips available that can be used to add texture to your cookies. In this project, you will use a grass tip to pipe fur onto cute little teddy bears.

Method

1. Hold the piping bag filled with the dark brown royal icing perpendicular to the cookie, with the tip just above the surface. Squeeze the piping bag while lifting the tip up and away from the cookie to allow the icing to come out. Stop squeezing the piping bag when the icing strands reach the desired fur length, and pull the tip away.

2. Continue to pipe fur to cover the entire surface of the cookie. Remember to keep the clusters of fur close together so that the cookie underneath does not show through.

3. Leave the cookies to dry for about an hour and then use the light-brown royal icing in a piping bag fitted with a No 2 round decorating tip to pipe details on the ears, paws, feet, and face of each bear.

You will need

Materials: Teddy bear cookies • Dark-brown stiff-peak royal icing • Medium-peak royal icing—light brown, black • Fondant—pale pink, blue **Tools:** Teddy bear cutter or template (see page 139) • Piping bag for the dark-brown icing, fitted with a No 233 (multi-opening/grass) decorating tip • Piping bag for the light-brown royal icing, fitted with a No 2 round decorating tip • Piping bag for the black royal icing, fitted with a No 1 round decorating tip • Bow silicone mold

4. Allow the cookies to dry before piping black dots of royal icing with a No 1 round decorating tip to create the eyes and nose.

5. To make the bows, press a small ball of pale-pink or pale-blue fondant for each cookie into a bow silicone mold until the fondant is flush with the back of the mold. Flex the mold to remove the bow, and then attach it to a bear using a small dot of royal icing.

In this project you will learn how to pipe layered shades of ruffles to create an ombré or "shaded" effect on little egg-shaped cookies.

Ombré Ruffle Eggs

You will need

Materials: Egg-shaped cookies • Stiff-peak white royal icing • Pink and green food-coloring gel • Pink fondant • Edible glue
Tools: Egg-shaped cutter or template (see page 138) • 9–12 x piping bags (one for each shade of icing) • Small petal decorating tip (e.g. No 103) • Bow silicone mold • Fine paintbrush • Small knife

Method

To make the pink ombré eggs

1. Divide the white royal icing between 3 bowls. In one bowl, add pink food-coloring gel to color the icing to a dark pink. Spoon a quarter of the dark pink icing into a piping bag fitted with a small petal decorating tip. Pipe a line of dark-pink ruffles along the base of half of the cookies.

2. Next, mix a tablespoon of white royal icing into the dark-pink icing in the bowl to make a slightly lighter shade of pink. Spoon a quarter of this pink icing into a clean piping bag fitted with a small petal decorating tip. Pipe a row of pink ruffles above the first row of ruffles on half of the cookies.

3. Continue to repeat step 2, each time adding a small amount of white royal icing to the remaining pink icing in the bowl to make a lighter shade, until the entire cookie surface is covered. Aim to pipe at least 5 different shades of pink onto the cookie. This will create an ombré effect, with the darkest shade of pink at the bottom and the lightest shade at the top. Allow the cookie to dry for at least 4 hours (preferably overnight) before serving.

Tip Practice piping ruffles on parchment paper before piping onto your cookie.

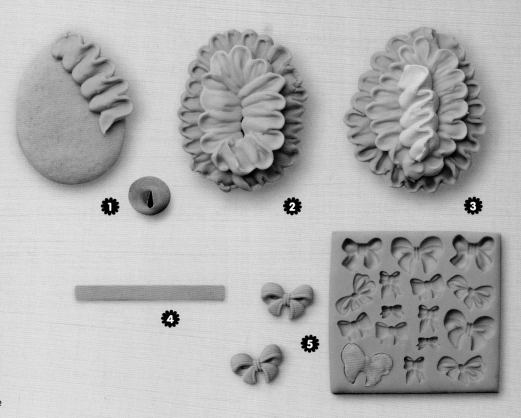

Method

To make the green ombré eggs

1. Add green food-coloring gel to one bowl of white royal icing to color the icing to a dark green. Spoon a quarter of the dark-green icing into a piping bag fitted with a small petal decorating tip. Pipe a border of dark green ruffles around the edge of half of the cookies.

2. Next, mix a tablespoon of white royal icing into the dark-green icing in the bowl to make a slightly lighter shade of green. Spoon a quarter of this green icing into a clean piping bag fitted with a petal decorating tip. Pipe green ruffles inside the edge of the first row of ruffles.

3. Add a small amount of white royal icing to the remaining green icing in the bowl to make a lighter shade of green. Use this icing to pipe a vertical strip of ruffles in the center of the egg. Allow the icing to dry for at least 4 hours (preferably overnight) before adding any decorations.

4. If desired, create a bow by rolling out a thin pink fondant strip and using a knife to trim it to the width of the center of the egg. Apply edible glue to the back of the strip with a fine paintbrush, then attach it across the center of the egg.

5. Create a bow by pressing a small ball of pink fondant into a bow silicone mold. Ensure the fondant is flush with the back of the mold, and then flex the mold to remove the bow. Attach a bow to the center of each pink strip, using edible glue to secure it in place.

TECHNIQUE IN FOCUS
Piping ruffles

❀ Petal tips are shaped like teardrops and have a broad and a narrow end. When piping a line of ruffles or a ruffle border, the broad end of the decorating tip should touch the cookie and the narrow end should point out off the edge of the cookie.

❀ Gently squeeze the icing out of the piping bag while moving the tip up and down (that is, out toward the edge of the cookie and then back in toward the center of the cookie) as you pipe around the edge of the cookie or in a line.

In this project you will make little three-dimensional gingerbread baskets filled with miniature strawberry cookies. If you don't fancy strawberries, try filling the basket with candy, mini chocolate eggs, or little flower-shaped cookies to create a lovely springtime gift or a treat for Easter.

Strawberry Baskets

You will need

Materials: Gingerbread dough (chilled) • White fondant • Vanilla dough (chilled) • Medium-peak royal icing—white, red, green • Thinned red royal icing in a squeeze bottle **Tools:** Non-stick rolling pin • Circle cutters (¾ in. [2 cm], 1 in. [2.5 cm], 1½ in. [4 cm], 1¾ in. [4.5 cm], and 2 in. [5 cm] in diameter) • Palette knife • Small heart cutter • Small star cutter • 3 x piping bags for the royal icing, fitted with No 2 round decorating tips

. . . .

Method

To make the baskets

1. Using a non-stick rolling pin, roll out the chilled gingerbread dough on a non-stick surface until it is ¼ in. (5 mm) in thickness. Use the 1 in. (2.5 cm), 1½ in. (4 cm), 1¾ in. (4.5 cm), and 2 in. (5 cm) circle cutters to cut out four different-sized rounds of dough. Use the ¾ in. (2 cm) circle cutter to cut out the center from the 1½ in. (4 cm) round cookie. Use the 1 in. (2.5 cm) cutter to cut out the center from the 1¾ in. (4.5 cm) round cookie, and use the 1½ in. (4 cm) cutter to cut out the center of the 2 in. (5 cm) round cookie. You will have one round cookie, and three different-sized cookie rings to make one basket.

To make the basket handle, roll a cylinder of gingerbread dough to approximately 4 in. (10 cm) in length and shape it into an arch. Use a palette knife to transfer the cookies onto a prepared baking sheet, and then bake them according to the dough recipe. Allow the cookies to cool completely before assembling.

2. To assemble the basket, place the 1 in. (2.5 cm) round cookie on a surface, then use white royal icing to attach the smallest ring on top of it.

3. Next use white royal icing to attach the medium ring on top of the small ring, followed by the large ring on top of the medium ring.

4. Complete the basket by attaching the handle to the top of the basket with white royal icing. It may be necessary to hold the handle in position for a few minutes until the royal icing starts to set. Allow the basket to dry for at least an hour before adding decorations.

5. If desired, use a non-stick rolling pin to roll out some white fondant on a non-stick surface to make a napkin to line the basket. It doesn't matter if the edges of the fondant are jagged, as it helps to give the fondant a more realistic fabric effect.

6. Gently drape the fondant into the basket. The basket is now ready to fill with goodies.

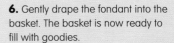

To make the strawberry cookies

7. To make mini strawberries to fill the basket, roll out chilled vanilla dough using a non-stick rolling pin until it is ¼ in. (5 mm) in thickness. Use a small heart cutter and a small star cutter to cut out one heart and one star for each strawberry.

8. Use the bottom half of the small star cutter to cut out the top of each heart, then insert the cut-out stars into the gap. This will form the shape of a strawberry.

9. Use a palette knife to transfer the cookies to a prepared baking sheet, and then bake according to the dough recipe. Allow the cookies to cool completely before decorating.

10. To decorate, pipe the outline of each strawberry with medium-peak red royal icing bag in a piping bag fitted with a No 2 round decorating tip, then flood inside the outline with the thinned red royal icing in the squeeze bottle. Allow the cookies to dry for about an hour.

11. Once dry, use green medium-peak royal icing in a piping bag fitted with a No 2 round decorating tip to pipe little green leaves on the top of each strawberry.

12. Lastly, pipe little seeds onto each strawberry, using medium-peak red royal icing in a piping bag fitted with a No 2 round decorating tip.

13. Leave the cookies to dry for at least an hour, then place them in the basket.

Method

1. Using a non-stick rolling pin, roll out the chilled cookie dough to an even thickness on a non-stick surface. Cut out different shapes from the dough using a selection of small cutters. You should aim to cut out at least 4 to 5 shapes for each bracelet. Place the shapes, evenly spaced, on a lined baking sheet.

2. Press the tip of a No 16 round decorating tip into the center of each cookie to cut out a hole from the middle. Place the sheet of cookies in a freezer for at least 10 minutes to chill, before baking according to the dough recipe. Allow the cookies to cool completely before decorating.

Charm Bracelets

In this project, you will make sweet little cookies that can be strung together to make charm bracelets—a great craft activity for a child's birthday party. While I have used hearts, butterflies, and flowers, any small shape can be used. Simply create a large batch of charms and place them in bowls on a table with an assortment of ribbons. The children will love threading the ribbons through the charms and making their own individual bracelets and accessories.

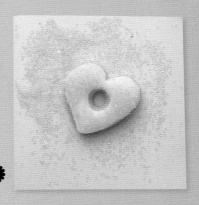

3. Using white royal icing in a piping bag fitted with a No 2 round decorating tip, pipe an outline around each cookie, and around each hole in the center.

4. Apply the thinned white royal icing from the squeeze bottle into the outlined section on each cookie to flood it with royal icing. Sometimes air bubbles may appear in the royal icing, so have a pin or toothpick on hand to pop them.

5. While the icing is still wet, lightly sprinkle the top of each cookie with either nonpareils or sanding sugar. You can leave the cookies plain if you prefer.

6. Leave the cookies to dry for at least 6 hours (preferably overnight). Once dry, turn them over and decorate the other side by repeating steps 3 to 5.

You will need

Materials: Vanilla cookie dough (chilled) • Medium-peak white royal icing • Thinned white royal icing in a squeeze bottle • Pastel-colored sanding sugar and nonpareils (e.g. pink, green) **Tools:** Non-stick rolling pin • Small cookie cutters in assorted shapes of your choice (e.g. hearts, flowers) or templates (see page 139) • No 16 round decorating tip • Piping bag for the medium-peak royal icing, fitted with a No 2 round decorating tip • Pin or toothpick • Ribbon

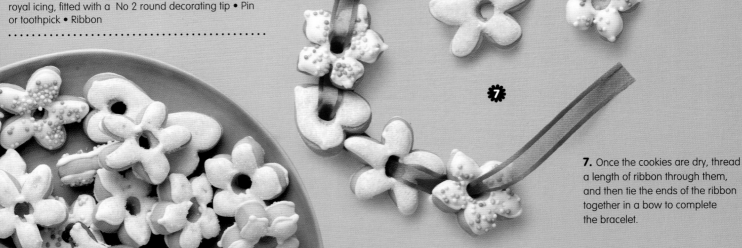

7. Once the cookies are dry, thread a length of ribbon through them, and then tie the ends of the ribbon together in a bow to complete the bracelet.

In this project, you will learn how to create pretty marbled patterns simply using royal icing and a toothpick.

Marbled Flowers

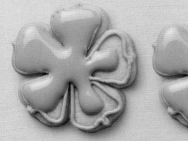

Method

1. Pipe an outline of medium-peak lilac royal icing around a cookie, following the line of each petal as a guide, using a No 2 round decorating tip.

2. Flood the inside of each outlined cookie, using thinned lilac royal icing in a squeeze bottle. Be careful not to overfill the cookies, otherwise the royal icing will leak over the edge of the outline. Sometimes air bubbles may appear in the royal icing, so have a pin or toothpick on hand to pop them.

3. While the lilac icing is still wet, squeeze a drop of thinned white royal icing from a squeeze bottle into the center of the flower.

You will need

Materials: 5-petal flower cookies approximately 1½ in. (4.5 cm) in width • Medium-peak royal icing—white and lilac • Thinned lilac, white, and yellow royal icing in squeeze bottles **Tools:** 5-petal flower cutter or template (see page 139) • Piping bags for the medium-peak royal icing, fitted with No 2 round decorating tips • Toothpick

. . . .

TECHNIQUE IN FOCUS:
Creating marbled patterns with royal icing

❋ Outline a cookie with medium-peak royal icing, using a piping bag fitted with a No 2 round decorating tip.

❋ Use squeeze bottles to pipe alternate lines of 2 different-colored thinned royal icings inside the outline of the cookie.

❋ Alternatively, you can flood the whole of the inside of the outline with 1 color of thinned icing, and then pipe lines of a different-colored thinned icing over the top of the icing while it is still wet.

❋ Starting at one edge of the top of the cookie, take a toothpick and drag it vertically down the length of the cookie through all of the stripes. When you reach the bottom of the cookie, move the toothpick slightly away from the line you have just made, and then drag it back up through the icing to the top of the cookie. Make sure there is some distance between this new line and the first line you created, so that the patterns do not bleed into each other.

❋ Continue to drag the toothpick up and down through the icing to create the marbled pattern.

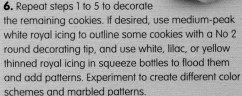

4. Take a clean toothpick and drag it from the center of the white dot into the base of one of the lilac petals. Lift the toothpick out of the icing and then place it back in the center of the white dot again and drag it toward a different petal. Continue to do this until the white icing has been dragged into the base of each petal on the flower.

5. The cookie can be left to dry, or if desired, more marbled patterns can be added to the tip of each petal. Try adding 3 or 4 small dots of thinned white icing at the tip of each petal, then use a toothpick to drag the white icing dots toward the center of the cookie.

6. Repeat steps 1 to 5 to decorate the remaining cookies. If desired, use medium-peak white royal icing to outline some cookies with a No 2 round decorating tip, and use white, lilac, or yellow thinned royal icing in squeeze bottles to flood them and add patterns. Experiment to create different color schemes and marbled patterns.

7. Leave the cookies to dry for at least 6 hours (preferably overnight) before serving.

In this project, you will learn how to create a cross-stitch effect on your cookies. You can easily adjust the technique to pipe more intricate patterns, using cross-stitch sewing patterns to guide your design. This technique requires a bit of patience as it can be time consuming to create each cookie depending on how intricate you make your cross-stitch design. But the overall effect is so delicate and lovely that it's definitely worth the time and effort!

Sew Pretty

You will need

Materials: Heart cookies (gingerbread or chocolate cookies will provide a nice contrast to the design—I have used hearts that are 2½ in. [6 cm] in width at the widest point) • Medium-peak white royal icing **Tools:** Scribing tool • Fine paintbrush • Piping bag for the royal icing, fitted with a No 1 round decorating tip

· ·

Tips

❀ If some of your royal icing lines break during piping, use a fine paintbrush to scrape them off from the cookie surface and repipe them.

❀ If you have a steady hand, try piping miniature crosses with a No 0 round decorating tip in the grids instead of dots.

Method

1. Use a scribing tool to mark the shape of the heart at least ¼ in. (5 mm) from the edge of the cookie. Brush away any cookie crumbs.

3. Next, pipe evenly spaced vertical lines of white royal icing across the heart to create a gridlike pattern. The cookie is now ready for your cross-stitch pattern to be added.

2. Within the outline, pipe evenly spaced straight lines of white royal icing horizontally across the heart, using a No 1 round decorating tip.

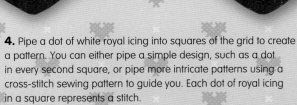

4. Pipe a dot of white royal icing into squares of the grid to create a pattern. You can either pipe a simple design, such as a dot in every second square, or pipe more intricate patterns using a cross-stitch sewing pattern to guide you. Each dot of royal icing in a square represents a stitch.

5. Once the design is complete, pipe dots of royal icing around the edge of the grid to cover any uneven edges. Repeat the steps to pipe a cross-stitch design on each cookie.

By using royal icing to assemble square cookies into a cube, you can make a sweet little edible box. This treat is perfect to hold more cookies or candy (or perhaps the charm bracelet cookies on page 94), and would make a lovely gift for someone special. While I have added quite intricate flourishes to the outside of the box, you can easily simplify the design and omit any filigree work to make a more contemporary box. Alternatively, you can personalize the box by piping the name or monogram of the recipient onto the lid.

Byzantine Jewelry Box

You will need

Materials: 6 x square cookies for each box (2⅝ in. [6.5 cm] in width) • Medium-peak royal icing—purple, peach, white • Thinned purple royal icing in a squeeze bottle • Gold edible paint or gold edible luster dust mixed with water or clear alcohol to make a paint (optional) • White gum paste (optional) **Tools:** 2 x piping bags fitted with No 2 round decorating tips • Pin or toothpick • Fine paintbrush • Lock and key silicone molds (optional) • Ornate heart or brooch silicone mold (optional)

Method
Decorating the cookies with royal icing

1. Each box will require 6 squares, but there is no need to decorate the square that will be the base of the jewelry box, as you won't be able to see it. For each box, pipe an outline around 5 square cookies, using medium-peak purple royal icing in a piping bag fitted with a No 2 round decorating tip.

2. Apply the thinned purple royal icing in the squeeze bottle into the outlined section on each cookie to flood it with royal icing. Be careful not to overfill the cookie, otherwise the royal icing will leak over the edge of the outline. Sometimes air bubbles may appear in the royal icing, so have a pin or toothpick on hand to pop them.

3. Leave the cookies to dry for at least 6 hours (preferably overnight) before assembling the box or adding further decorations.

Tip Any molded decorations can be made in advance and stored at room temperature in a box once the paint has dried.

Adding the details

4. If you would like to decorate the box, pipe a filigree border around the edge of each purple square, using medium-peak peach royal icing in a piping bag fitted with a No 2 round decorating tip. You can pipe any design that you like, such as scrolls, snail trails, or a row of dots.

5. I have piped a series of connected scroll-like U-shapes around the border, followed by small dots on the join of each U-shape. Allow the filigree work to dry for at least 2 hours.

6. Once the squares are dry, the filigree patterns can be painted with gold edible paint using a fine paintbrush.

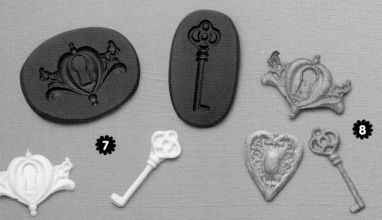

7. If desired, you can use silicone molds to create a brooch or motif to attach to the lid, and a lock to go on one side of the box (to denote the front). In my design I have made an ornate heart for the lid, a lock for the front, and a key. The shapes are made by pressing a small ball of

white gum paste into heart, lock, and key silicone molds. Ensure that the gum paste is flush with the back of the molds, then flex them to remove the shapes. If the gum paste sticks to the mold, grease it with some vegetable fat (shortening) before adding the gum paste.

8. Allow the heart, lock, and key to firm for 30 minutes, then paint them with gold edible paint. Leave them to dry completely for at least an hour before attaching the heart and lock to the lid and box with a small dot of royal icing.

Continued next page

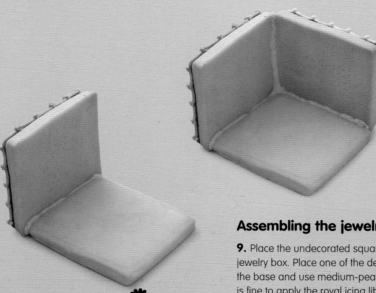

Assembling the jewelry box

9. Place the undecorated square on a flat surface. This will be the base of the jewelry box. Place one of the decorated squares perpendicular to one edge of the base and use medium-peak white royal icing to join the pieces together. It is fine to apply the royal icing liberally. If you use too much and it oozes out of the joins, you can easily wipe off any excess with a dry fine paintbrush.

11. To add extra strength to the box, pipe a snail trail vertically along the joins on the outside of the box, using medium-peak white royal icing in a piping bag fitted with a No 2 round decorating tip (see page 31). Allow the snail trail to dry for at least 2 hours.

12. If desired, paint the snail trail with gold edible paint, using a fine paintbrush to complete the design.

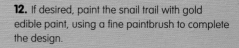

10. Next attach the remaining 3 sides to the base, using white royal icing to secure them in place. It may be necessary to hold each side upright for a few minutes after joining it to the base until the royal icing firms up enough for you to be able to let go without it falling over.

13. Once the jewelry box is dry, fill it with candy or small cookies, if desired.

Monochrome Lacework

Learn how to use simple piping techniques to create delicate lace patterns.

You will need

Materials: Gray fondant • Round cookies approximately 2½ in. (6 cm) in diameter • Clear piping gel • Medium-peak white royal icing **Tools:** Non-stick rolling pin • Circle cutters 2½ in. (6 cm), 1¾ in. (4.5 cm) and 1 in. (2.5 cm) in diameter • Fine paintbrush • Palette knife • Piping bag for the royal icing, fitted with a No 1 round decorating tip

Method

1. Using a non-stick rolling pin, roll out the gray fondant on a non-stick surface to approximately ⅛ in. (3 mm) in thickness. Use the largest circle cutter to cut out rounds of fondant to cover the cookies.

2. Apply a thin layer of piping gel to the surface of each cookie, using a fine paintbrush. Carefully lift the fondant rounds with a palette knife and place them on top of the cookies. The piping gel will act as glue and attach the fondant to the cookie.

3. Gently rub a finger around the edge of the fondant to achieve a smooth finish.

4. Immediately after attaching the fondant to the cookie, center the medium and small circle cutters gently on the surface of each cookie and then press them lightly into the fondant. Remove the cutters to reveal two embossed rings that will act as templates for the piping work.

5. Using medium-peak white royal icing in a piping bag fitted with a No 1 round decorating tip, pipe over the top of each embossed ring.

6. Next, pipe little white swags (U-shapes) around each ring.

7. Pipe little dots of royal icing on the inside rim of the inner circle. If the dots have a pointy peak, use a damp paintbrush to gently soften them.

8. If you would like to add a more intricate design, pipe dots vertically under the swags on the inner circle of the cookie to join the design to the outer piped circle. Alternatively, you can pipe another row of swags or a different design to join the inner and outer piped circles together.

9. To give the cookie a professional finish, pipe a snail trail around the edge of each cookie (see page 31) before leaving them to dry for at least 4 hours (preferably overnight).

Tip You can make the lace patterns as simple or detailed as you wish. Look at old crocheted doilies for design inspiration.

Wafer Paper

Wafer paper is a versatile medium that can be used to make delicate decorations or printed with edible ink to create personalized motifs. Simply attach wafer paper to dry cookies with edible glue. Once you have decorated your cookies, be sure to keep them away from water, as wafer paper will dissolve when wet.

Whimsical Water Lilies

As an alternative to fondant, cookies can be decorated with delicate wafer paper. In this project, you will learn how to make pretty water lilies to adorn lily-pad cookies.

You will need

Materials: White wafer paper • Edible luster dusts (pink and yellow) • Round cookies approximately 2½ in. (6 cm) in diameter • Medium-peak green royal icing • Thinned green royal icing in a squeeze bottle **Tools:** Scissors • Fine paintbrush • Soft paintbrush • Tweezers • Piping bag for the royal icing, fitted with a No 2 round decorating tip • Pin or toothpick

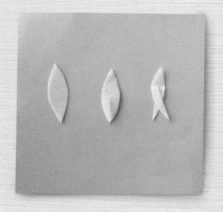

Method

1. Use the templates (see page 139) to cut out 12 large, 10 medium, and 8 small petals from white wafer paper. Starting at the base of each petal, use scissors to cut a slit a third of the way up the center of each petal.

2. For each petal, use a damp, fine paintbrush to moisten one side of the cut section, cross it under the other section, and press down to secure it.

5. Cut a thin strip of wafer paper approximately 2 in. (5 cm) long. Use a soft paintbrush to dust the smooth side of the wafer paper with yellow edible luster dust. Shake off any excess dust.

6. Cut a fine fringe along one edge of the wafer paper with scissors. Moisten the base of the fringe and roll it up to form a stamen cluster. Press the base of the cluster tightly between your fingers to secure it.

7. Moisten the center of the water lily with a damp paintbrush, and then secure the stamen cluster in position with tweezers.

3. Moisten the bases of the large petals and arrange into a flower shape, ensuring that each petal overlaps the previous one. For the next layer, moisten the bases of the medium petals and place each one between two petals from the first layer, again ensuring that the medium petals overlap each other as they are added. Moisten the small petal bases and add, overlapping, in an upright position in the center of the water lily.

4. Allow the water lilies to dry and then use a soft paintbrush to color the edges of the petals with pink edible luster dust.

8. Pipe the outline of the lily pad onto each cookie, using medium-peak green royal icing in a piping bag fitted with a No 2 round decorating tip.

9. Apply the thinned green royal icing from the squeeze bottle into the outlined section on each cookie to flood it with royal icing. Be careful not to overfill the outline, otherwise the royal icing will leak over the edge. Sometimes air bubbles may appear in the royal icing, so have a pin or toothpick on hand to pop them. Leave the cookies to dry for at least 6 hours before attaching the water lilies to them with a small amount of royal icing.

Tip Leave the cookies to dry under a lamp to achieve a shiny surface.

Perfume Bottles

In this project, you will learn how to use printed wafer-paper labels to decorate perfume bottle cookies.

You will need

Materials: Cookie dough (chilled)
• Medium-peak white royal icing
• Food-coloring gel—pink, purple
• Wafer paper printed with vintage perfume labels • Gold edible luster dust • Edible glue • Clear alcohol
Tools: Non-stick rolling pin • Perfume bottle templates (see page 140)
• Small sharp knife • 3 x piping bags for the royal icing, fitted with No 2 round decorating tips • 3 x squeeze bottles • Pin or toothpick • Scissors
• Fine paintbrush

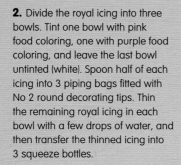

Method

1. Using a non-stick rolling pin, roll out the chilled cookie dough on a non-stick surface to approximately ¼ in. (5 mm) in thickness. Place the perfume bottle templates on the dough and use a knife to cut around each one. Transfer the perfume bottles onto a lined baking sheet and bake them in a preheated oven, following the dough recipe. Allow the cookies to cool before decorating.

2. Divide the royal icing into three bowls. Tint one bowl with pink food coloring, one with purple food coloring, and leave the last bowl untinted (white). Spoon half of each icing into 3 piping bags fitted with No 2 round decorating tips. Thin the remaining royal icing in each bowl with a few drops of water, and then transfer the thinned icing into 3 squeeze bottles.

3. Use the pink and purple royal icing in the piping bags to pipe a border around each perfume bottle cookie. Use the white royal icing in the piping bag to pipe the border of each perfume bottle lid.

4. Squeeze the thinned pink and purple royal icing in the squeeze bottles into the corresponding outlined section on each cookie to flood it with royal icing. Be careful not to overfill the outline, otherwise the royal icing will leak over the edge. Sometimes air bubbles may appear in the royal icing, so have a pin or toothpick on hand to pop them.

5. Squeeze the thinned white royal icing into the outlined section of each perfume bottle lid until it is completely covered.

6. Leave the cookies to dry. Pipe lines of medium-peak white royal icing using a No 2 round decorating tip onto each perfume bottle lid to give it a textured or three-dimensional look. Allow the icing to dry for about an hour.

7. Mix a small amount of gold luster dust with clear alcohol (such as vodka) in a small bowl or paint palette well, until it reaches the consistency of paint. Use a very fine paintbrush to apply the gold paint to the perfume bottle lids. Allow the paint to dry for about 30 minutes.

8. Use a small pair of scissors to cut out the wafer paper labels. Moisten the back of the labels with a little bit of edible glue, then attach them to the center of each cookie.

There are lots of fabulous paper punches available in craft stores. Although they have been designed to cut cardboard and paper, they are also useful for shaping wafer paper. In this project, you will learn how to use a paper punch to make lacelike ribbon for your cookies.

Frilly Lace Fancies

Method
1. Using pale-blue medium-peak royal icing in a piping bag fitted with a No 2 round decorating tip, pipe an outline around each cookie.

You will need
Materials: Medium-peak pale-blue royal icing • Thinned pale-blue royal icing in a squeeze bottle • White wafer paper • Square cookies 2½ in. (6 cm) in width • White fondant • Edible pearls
Tools: Piping bag for the royal icing, fitted with a No 2 round decorating tip • Pin or toothpick • Scissors • Non-stick rolling pin • Paper punch (e.g. doily lace-edge paper punch) • Small knife • Fine paintbrush

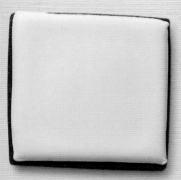

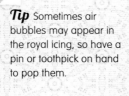

Tip Sometimes air bubbles may appear in the royal icing, so have a pin or toothpick on hand to pop them.

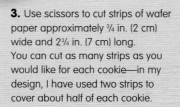

2. Apply the thinned pale-blue royal icing from the squeeze bottle into the outlined section on each cookie to flood it with royal icing. Be careful not to overfill the cookie, otherwise the royal icing will leak over the edge of the outline. Leave the cookies to dry for at least 6 hours (preferably overnight).

3. Use scissors to cut strips of wafer paper approximately ¾ in. (2 cm) wide and 2¾ in. (7 cm) long. You can cut as many strips as you would like for each cookie—in my design, I have used two strips to cover about half of each cookie.

4. Use an edge paper punch to cut out a pattern from one long edge of each strip. Make enough strips to decorate your cookies in your chosen design.

5. Moisten the back of the top edge of each strip with a tiny amount of water and then attach them on top of each cookie, ensuring that each strip overlaps the previous strip. It is easiest to place the first strip in the center of the cookie, and then attach the other strip to the left of the first strip, making sure that it is positioned so that it reaches the edge of the cookie. Use scissors to trim the straight edges of each strip so they are flush with the edge of the cookie.

6. Roll out the white fondant on a non-stick surface with a non-stick rolling pin. Use a knife to cut out a thin strip approximately ½ in. (1 cm) wide and 2¾ in. (7 cm) long for each cookie. Moisten the back of each strip with a small amount of water and attach them along the left edge of each cookie, on top of the straight edge of the wafer-paper strip.

7. To make the bows, roll out the remaining fondant and cut out 2 small strips approximately ½ in. (1 cm) wide and 1 in. (2.5 cm) long for each cookie. Fold the ends of the strips toward each other to make loops, securing them with a moistened paintbrush. Attach 2 loops, with their ends joining, on top of each white fondant strip with a dot of royal icing.

8. Arrange 6 edible pearls in the shape of a round brooch in between the 2 loops (in the center of the bow), and use royal icing to secure them in place.

In this project, you will make little photo frame cookies that can be used to display any image you desire. While I have used preprinted wafer-paper sheets, you could have your photographs printed onto plain wafer paper with edible ink, and then insert them into the frames instead.

Pretty as a Picture

You will need

Materials: Cookie dough (chilled) • Medium-peak royal icing—white, peach • Thinned white and peach royal icing in squeeze bottles • Edible gold paint (or edible gold luster dust mixed with water or clear alcohol to make a paint) • Wafer paper printed with a design or photos of your choice • Edible glue
Tools: Large non-stick rolling pin • 2 square cutters (2¾ in. [7 cm] and 2 in. [5 cm] in width) • Palette knife • Piping bags for the medium-peak royal icing, fitted with No 2 round decorating tips • Fine paintbrush • Scissors

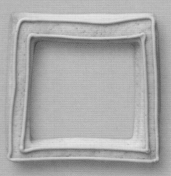

6. Pipe an outline around the frame cookies, using medium-peak peach royal icing in a piping bag fitted with a No 2 round decorating tip.

7. Apply thinned peach royal icing from the squeeze bottle into the outlined section of each frame cookie to flood it with royal icing. Allow the square and frame cookies to dry for at least 6 hours (preferably overnight).

 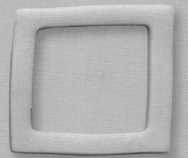  

Method
Making the frames

1. Using a non-stick rolling pin, roll out the chilled cookie dough on a non-stick surface to approximately ¼ in. (5 mm) in thickness. Use the larger square cutter to cut out 2 squares for each cookie.

2. Use the smaller square cutter to cut out the middle from half of the larger squares. This will create a frame shape.

3. Use a palette knife to transfer the squares and frames onto a lined baking sheet and bake them in a preheated oven, following the dough recipe. Allow the cookies to cool before decorating.

Decorating the frames

4. Pipe the outline of the square cookies, using medium-peak white royal icing in a piping bag fitted with a No 2 round decorating tip.

5. Apply thinned white royal icing from the squeeze bottle into the outlined section on each square cookie to flood it with royal icing.

> ***Tip*** Attach a loop of satin ribbon to the back of each cookie using royal icing to secure it in place. This will enable you to hang the frames—a sweet idea for Christmas tree decorations.

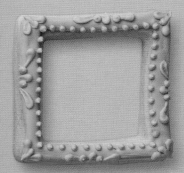   

8. If desired, once the frame cookies are dry, use medium-peak peach royal icing in a piping bag fitted with a No 2 round decorating tip to pipe flourishes and dots onto each cookie to create ornate frames.

9. Allow the icing to dry for about an hour and then paint each frame with gold edible paint. Leave the frames to one side to dry for a few minutes.

10. Use a small pair of scissors to cut out the wafer-paper images so that they are no larger than the white squares. Moisten the back of the images with edible glue, then attach them on top of each white square cookie.

11. Use a small amount of royal icing to stick the gold-frame cookies on top of the wafer-paper images, so that they are aligned with the edges of the square cookies underneath.

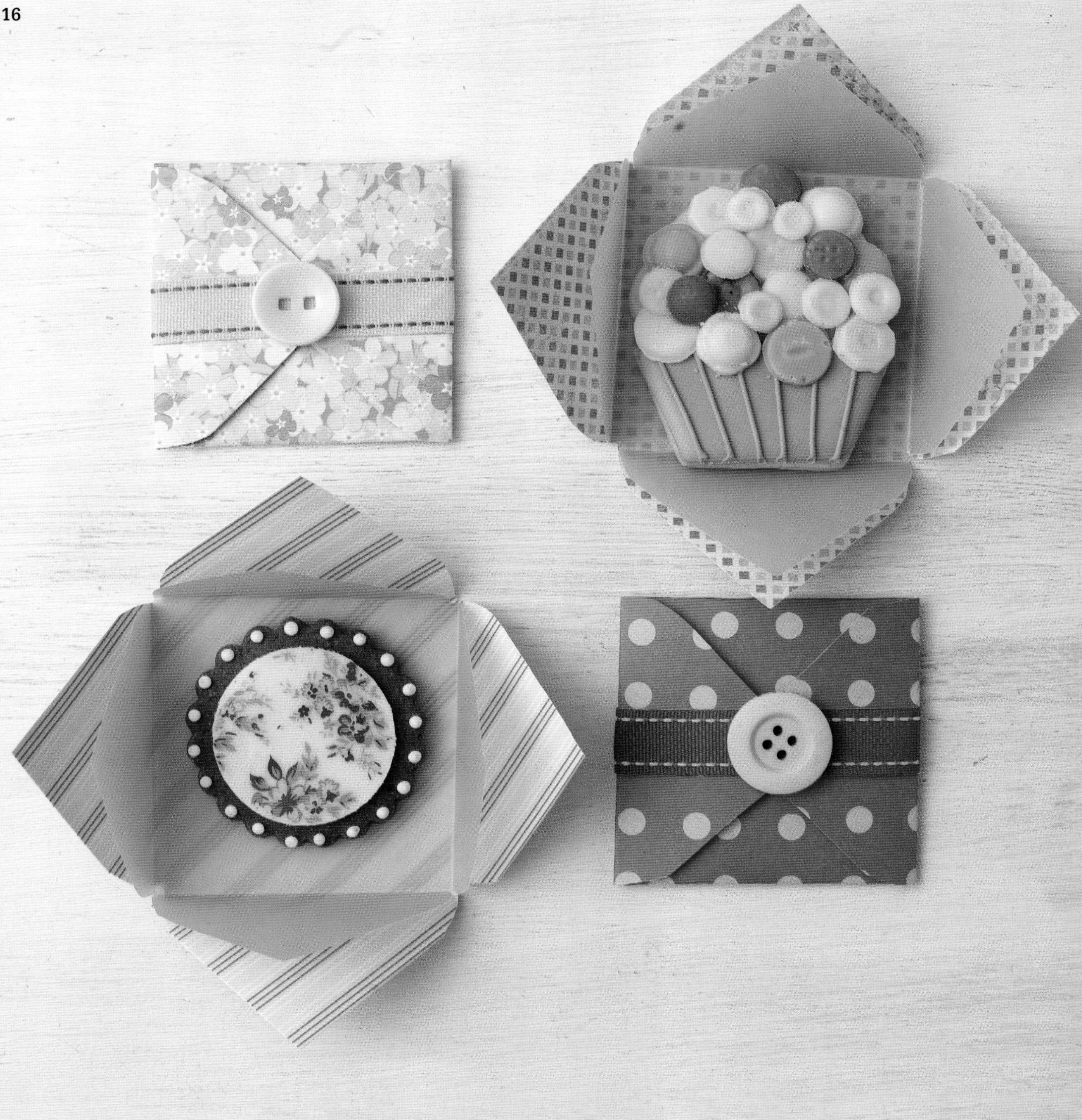

Chocolate

Chocolate decorations are simple to make if you have silicone or plastic molds on hand. Simply pour melted chocolate or candy wafers into the molds, tap them against the work surface to remove any air bubbles, and then place them in the freezer to set. After about 10 minutes, the chocolate should easily pop out when the molds are flexed. Attach them to cookies with a dab of melted chocolate.

In this project, you will learn how to use candy wafers and molds to make pretty, colored chocolate buttons to decorate cupcake cookies.

Cute Cupcakes

You will need

Materials: Colored candy wafers (e.g. green, pink, turquoise, purple, yellow) • Cupcake cookies • Medium-peak purple royal icing • Thinned purple royal icing in a squeeze bottle **Tools:** Cupcake cutter or template (see page 140) • Button mold • Silicone spatula • Piping bag for the medium-peak royal icing, fitted with a No 2 round decorating tip

Method

1. Place roughly chopped candy wafers (single color) in a microwave-safe bowl. Microwave the candy wafers on 50 percent power for 1 minute, then stir well. Continue to microwave for 15–30 second intervals, stirring well after each interval until smooth. Repeat the process to melt the other candy wafers in separate bowls.

2. Use a teaspoon to carefully fill the melted candy into the different buttons in the mold. After filling the buttons, tap the mold on a hard surface to settle the candy, and remove any trapped air. If necessary, level the candy by scraping away the excess with a silicone spatula.

4. Pipe an outline around the base of each cupcake cookie (for the cupcake case), using medium-peak purple royal icing in a piping bag fitted with a No 2 round decorating tip.

5. Apply the thinned purple royal icing from the squeeze bottle into the outlined section on each cookie to flood it with royal icing. Be careful not to overfill the cookie, otherwise the royal icing will leak over the edge of the outline.

6. Leave the cookies to dry for at least 6 hours (preferably overnight). If desired, pipe vertical lines of medium-peak purple royal icing onto the cupcake cases, using a No 2 round decorating tip.

7. Once the cookies have dried, use small dots of royal icing to stick the buttons on top of each cupcake in a clustered pattern, to resemble the frosting on a cupcake.

3. After the candy has hardened at room temperature, chill the mold in a refrigerator for approximately 10 minutes. Turn the mold upside down and press on the back of the cavities to release the buttons.

8. Continue to add buttons until the tops of the cupcake cookies are covered. Leave them to dry for a few minutes before serving.

Method

1. Place roughly chopped white candy wafers (or white chocolate) in a microwave-safe bowl. Microwave the candy wafers on 50 percent power for 1 minute, then stir well. Continue to microwave for 15–30 second intervals, stirring well after each interval until smooth. Repeat the process to melt the pink candy wafers. If using white chocolate instead, pour a third of the melted chocolate into a bowl and then tint it with two drops of pink food coloring.

2. Use a thin paintbrush to carefully paint the melted pink chocolate into the mold design. After filling each design, tap the mold on a hard surface to settle the chocolate and remove any trapped air. Use a small knife to scrape away any chocolate that has gone outside of the design.

3. Allow the painted design to cool at room temperature, then fill the mold cavities one third full with the white chocolate. Tap the mold gently on a hard surface to remove any trapped air.

Peppermint Treats

In this project, you will learn how to use candy wafers and cookie molds to make pretty coated Oreo cookies.

Presentation tip

Wrap the cookies in cellophane secured with pretty bows to package them like peppermint candies.

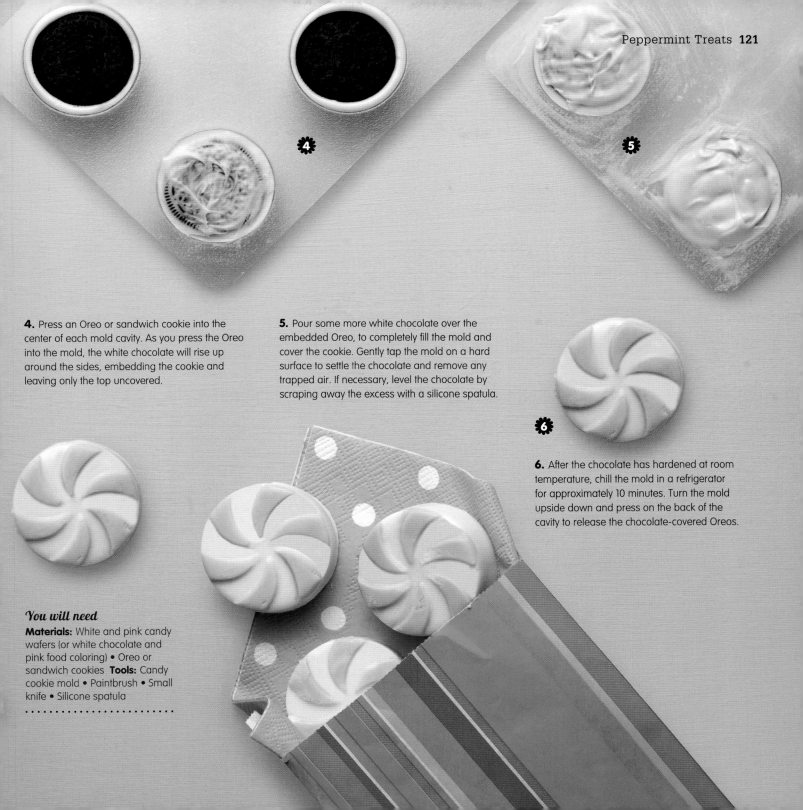

4. Press an Oreo or sandwich cookie into the center of each mold cavity. As you press the Oreo into the mold, the white chocolate will rise up around the sides, embedding the cookie and leaving only the top uncovered.

5. Pour some more white chocolate over the embedded Oreo, to completely fill the mold and cover the cookie. Gently tap the mold on a hard surface to settle the chocolate and remove any trapped air. If necessary, level the chocolate by scraping away the excess with a silicone spatula.

6. After the chocolate has hardened at room temperature, chill the mold in a refrigerator for approximately 10 minutes. Turn the mold upside down and press on the back of the cavity to release the chocolate-covered Oreos.

You will need

Materials: White and pink candy wafers (or white chocolate and pink food coloring) • Oreo or sandwich cookies **Tools:** Candy cookie mold • Paintbrush • Small knife • Silicone spatula

Chocolate transfer sheets (not to be confused with edible icing sheets) are strips of acetate that are embellished with cocoa butter. They are available in different colors and designs and are quick and simple to use to create patterned chocolate decorations.

Vintage Flowers

You will need

Materials: White candy wafers (or white chocolate) • Edible food coloring (pink and green) • Chocolate transfer sheet in design of your choice—I have used a floral pattern • Round fluted-edge cookies (2¼ in. [5.5 cm] in diameter) • Medium-peak white royal icing **Tools:** Spatula or palette knife • Circle cutter (2 in. [5 cm] in diameter) • Fluted circle cutter (2¼ in. [5.5 cm] in diameter) • Piping bag fitted with a No 2 round decorating tip

Tips

♣ Sharp, well-defined metal cutters work best to cut out chocolate transfers.

♣ The chocolate that surrounds the cut-out shapes is often oddly shaped, and is usually wasted. If using dark chocolate, you can save the leftover pieces and remelt them with additional dark chocolate (or dark-brown candy wafers). The small amount of cocoa butter and coloring from the transfer sheet will not be visible once it's remelted.

Method

1. Place the roughly chopped white candy wafers (or white chocolate) in a microwave-safe bowl. Microwave the candy wafers on 50 percent power for 1 minute, then stir well. Continue to microwave for 15–30 second intervals, stirring well after each interval until smooth. Divide the chocolate between 3 bowls and tint 1 bowl with 2 drops of pink food coloring and another bowl with 2 drops of green food coloring.

2. Cut the chocolate transfer sheet into 3 strips that are wider than the circle cutter. Place the chocolate transfer strips on a board, with the textured side of the transfer strip face up and the shiny (acetate) side face down. If the strip does not lie flat on the board, you can use a little bit of white chocolate to hold it in place.

3. Spoon some of the melted white chocolate onto 1 of the transfer strips and use a spatula or palette knife to spread the chocolate thinly over the top, so that all of the edges of the transfer strip are covered. Repeat the process to spread a thin layer of green and pink chocolate over the remaining transfer sheets.

4. Allow the chocolate to rest at room temperature for at least 5 minutes until it begins to set around the edges of each strip, but is not completely hardened or brittle.

5. Press the circle cutter firmly into the chocolate strips. After the desired number of rounds has been cut, allow the chocolate to set completely at room temperature or in a refrigerator before carefully peeling the rounds away from the acetate backing of the transfer sheet. Attach each chocolate round in the center of each cookie, using a thin spread of white melted chocolate to secure them in place.

6. Pipe dots of medium-peak white royal icing using a No 2 round decorating tip around the edge of the cookie to complete the design.

Method

1. Place roughly chopped white candy wafers (or white chocolate) in a microwave-safe bowl. Microwave the candy wafers on 50 percent power for 1 minute, then stir well. Continue to microwave for 15–30 second intervals, stirring well after each interval until smooth. Pour two-thirds of the melted chocolate into another bowl and tint with a few drops of pink food coloring. Tint the remaining white chocolate with a few drops of green food coloring.

2. Place the chocolate transfer sheets on a board or baking sheet lined with parchment paper, with the textured side of the transfer sheet face up and the shiny (acetate) side face down. If the sheet does not lie flat on the board, you can use a little bit of white chocolate to hold it in place. Spoon the melted pink chocolate onto the transfer sheet for the petals and use a spatula to spread the chocolate thinly over the top, so that all of the edges of the transfer sheet are covered. Repeat the process to spread a thin layer of green chocolate over the transfer sheet with the green design for the leaves.

3. Allow the chocolate to rest for around 5 minutes at room temperature until it begins to set around the edges of each strip, but is not completely hardened or brittle.

Dainty Corsages

In this project, you will build up heart-shaped cookies adorned with chocolate transfer sheets to make a three-dimensional flower, perfect as a table centerpiece or as a favor for guests at a wedding.

You will need

Materials: Candy wafers (white) or white chocolate • Pink and green edible food coloring gel • 2 chocolate transfer sheets (one with a green pattern for leaves, the other in a design of your choice for petals—I have used a lace pattern) • Stiff-peak white royal icing • Heart-shaped cookies—3 medium (1¾ in. [4.5 cm] in width at widest point) and 3 small (1¼ in. [3 cm] in width at widest point) for each corsage • Medium leaf cookies (up to 1½ in. [4 cm] in length)—6 for each corsage • Round cookies (1½ in. [4 cm] in diameter)—one for each corsage • Small blossom cookies (¾ in. [2 cm] in width)—one for each corsage • Pink sanding sugar **Tools:** Spatula • Heart cutters (same size as cookies) • Medium leaf cutter (same size as leaf cookies) • Piping bag for the royal icing, fitted with a No 2 round decorating tip

4. Press the heart cutters firmly into the pink patterned chocolate sheet to cut out 3 medium and 3 small hearts for each corsage. Press the leaf cutter into the green patterned chocolate strip to cut out 6 leaves for each corsage.

After the desired number of shapes has been cut, allow the chocolate to set completely at room temperature or in the refrigerator before carefully peeling the shapes away from the acetate backing of the transfer sheet.

5. Attach each chocolate shape to a corresponding cookie, using a thin spread of white melted chocolate to secure them in place.

6. Once they are dry, use royal icing to attach the 3 medium hearts, evenly spaced and at a 45-degree angle, to the round cookie. You will need to use balls of fondant or small objects to prop up the petals while they are drying.

7. Attach 3 green leaves in between the petals, again using fondant to hold them in position while they are drying.

8. Attach 3 small hearts on top of the medium hearts with royal icing, ensuring that they are evenly spaced. Add 3 leaves in between the petals. Again, you may need to use some fondant to hold the petals and leaves in position while they are drying.

9. Pipe white royal icing onto the surface of a small blossom cookie and then sprinkle pink sanding sugar over it while the icing is still wet. Allow the blossom to dry for a few minutes, then attach it into the small gap in the center of the corsage with a small dot of royal icing.

10. Once the petals and leaves have dried in position, remove the fondant supports. If desired, pipe dots of white royal icing (using a No 2 round decorating tip) around the edge of each petal and leaf to complete the design.

Tip Use smaller heart cutters to make smaller corsages. They can then be placed in little cellophane bags as gifts for friends.

The small blossom cookie can be decorated and placed on top of the corsage.

Quick Cookie Creations

With a few quick steps, you can create these pretty cookies in no time at all. Bake cookies in your desired shape and allow them to cool completely before decorating.

See also:
Tools & Equipment, page 12 and Core Techniques, page 16

Lustered Roses

1. Roll out some bright-pink fondant to ⅛ in. (3 mm) in thickness and cut out fluted squares with your cookie cutter. Secure the fondant on each cookie, using piping gel.

2. Place a rose stencil over the cookie and smear a little white vegetable fat (shortening) over the design. Apply gold edible luster dust with a broad paintbrush. Keep the stencil still as you dust.

3. Gently lift the stencil off the top of the cookie to reveal the lustered rose pattern.

Pink Frills

1. Using stiff-peak royal icing in a piping bag with a petal tip, hold the wider end of the tip touching the cookie and the thin end pointing toward the edge, and gently squeeze the piping bag while moving the tip up and down to pipe a ruffle.

2. Continue this technique while turning the cookie to pipe a ruffle around the edge. Pipe in rows until you reach the center.

3. Place 4 edible pearls in the center of the cookie using tweezers. Allow to dry for at least 4 hours.

Dainty Roses

1. Roll out some pale green fondant to ⅛ in. (3 mm) in thickness and cut out circles with your cookie cutter. Secure the fondant on each cookie, using piping gel.

2. Press pale pink gum paste into a rose silicone mold, lightly greased with white vegetable fat (shortening). Ensure the paste is flush with the back of the mold, then flex it to remove the finished rose.

3. Attach a rose in the center of each cookie with royal icing, then pipe small dots of pale-pink medium-peak royal icing around the edge, using a No 2 round decorating tip.

Cute as a Button!

1. Roll out pastel-colored fondant to ⅛ in. (3 mm) in thickness and cut out circles with your cookie cutter. Secure the fondant on each cookie, using piping gel.

2. Press a round cookie cutter, with a smaller diameter than the fondant covering, into the fondant to make the button rim. Use the end of a No 2 round decorating tip to imprint four holes for the button center.

3. Pipe medium-peak white royal icing between the holes for stitching.

Fairy Wands

1. Roll out pink fondant to ⅛ in. (3 mm) in thickness and cut out star shapes with your cookie cutter. Secure the fondant on each cookie, using piping gel.

2. Brush the fondant edges with piping gel, using a fine paintbrush, then sprinkle all over with edible glitter or sanding sugar.

3. Shake off the excess glitter, then tie a bow around the cookie stick.

Teabags

1. Use a template (see page 140) to cut out cookie dough in the shape of a teabag, and add a hole in the top of each cookie, using the end of a straw or a decorating tip, before baking.

2. Once the cookies have been baked and allowed to cool completely, dip their ends into melted dark chocolate and then place them on baking parchment at room temperature until the chocolate has set.

3. Tie ribbon or baker's twine through the hole of each cookie and attach a small label to the end of the ribbon, using double-sided tape to secure it in place.

Bunting Bliss

1. Roll out some pale blue fondant to ⅛ in. (3 mm) in thickness and cut out squares, using the same cutter used to form the cookies. Attach the fondant to the top of each cookie, using piping gel to hold it in place.

2. Cut out small isosceles triangles from patterned edible icing sheets and then attach them side by side to the fondant-covered cookie in an arched line with edible glue.

3. Pipe a string of white royal icing across the tops of the triangles to join them all together and complete the bunting. If desired, pipe a snail-trail border around each cookie with royal icing.

Doilies

1. Roll out some white fondant to ⅛ in. (3 mm) in thickness and cut out fluted rounds, using the same cutter used to form the cookies.

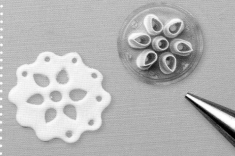

2. Use the end of No 1 and No 2 round decorating tips and eyelet cutters to cut out a doily pattern from the fondant rounds.

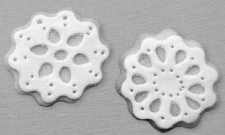

3. Attach the fondant to the surface of each cookie, using piping gel applied with a fine paintbrush to secure it in place.

Elegant Bows

1. Roll out some white fondant to ⅛ in. (3 mm) in thickness and cut out fluted squares, using the same cutter used to create the cookies. Attach the fondant to the top of each cookie, using piping gel to hold it in place.

2. Press an embossing stamp into the 4 corners of each fondant-covered cookie to create a filigree pattern.

3. Press some pink gum paste into a bow silicone mold that has been lightly greased with white vegetable fat (shortening). Ensure the paste is flush with the back of the mold, then flex the mold to remove the bow. Attach a bow to the center of each cookie, using royal icing.

Ribbon Roses

1. Pipe a green leaf with royal icing to cover the 5 petals on each blossom cookie. Allow the royal icing to dry.

2. Using a non-stick rolling pin, roll out thin rectangular strips of pink and lilac gum paste approximately 6 in. (15 cm) long and 1¼ in. (3 cm) wide. Use your fingers to roll each strip into a ribbon rose (see page 47), and then trim off any remaining gum paste with scissors.

3. Attach a ribbon rose to the center of each cookie, using royal icing.

Cameos

1. Roll out some duck-egg fondant to ⅛ in. (3 mm) in thickness and then gently press a textured mat over the top of the fondant to imprint it with polka dots. You may need to gently roll a non-stick rolling pin over the top of the mat while it is on the fondant to ensure that the pattern imprints evenly. Cut out fluted circles of the textured fondant using the cutter used to create the cookies.

2. Attach the fondant to the top of each cookie, using piping gel to hold it in place. Press some white gum paste into a small cameo silicone mold that has been lightly greased with white vegetable fat (shortening), and then flex the mold to remove the cameo. Attach a cameo to the center of each cookie with royal icing.

3. If desired, pipe small dots of white royal icing around the cameo, using a No 1 round decorating tip.

Recipes

A lot of cookie recipes I have used in the past make cookies that spread during baking. These recipes shown here, however, make cookies that will hold their shape. Like most cookie doughs, they also freeze well for at least a month, so you can wrap half of the dough in plastic wrap and save it for another day.

Chocolate Cookies

Ingredients *(makes 30 cookies)*

8 oz (225 g) unsalted butter (room temperature)

8 oz (225 g) light brown sugar

1 large egg (room temperature), beaten

15 oz (430 g) all-purpose flour

1 oz (30 g) unsweetened dark cocoa powder

Method

1. Place the butter and sugar in a mixing bowl and beat with an electric mixer until light and creamy. Gradually add in the egg until it is fully incorporated.

2. Sift in the flour and cocoa powder and mix on a slow speed until the ingredients begin to form a ball. Remove the dough from the bowl and wrap it in plastic wrap. Refrigerate for at least an hour until firm.

3. Preheat the oven to 350°F (180°C/gas mark 4). Allow the dough to soften slightly at room temperature, then roll it out on a lightly floured surface to the required thickness.

4. Cut out shapes using a cutter, then carefully lift the cookies with a palette knife and place them, evenly spaced, on a baking sheet lined with parchment paper. Bake the cookies for 10 to 12 minutes until they are just firm to the touch. Allow the cookies to completely cool on a wire rack before decorating.

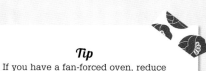

Tip
If you have a fan-forced oven, reduce the temperature stated in the recipes by 25°F (20°C).

Tip
Remember that larger cookies take longer to bake than smaller ones.

Vanilla Cookies

Ingredients *(makes 30 cookies)*

6 oz (175 g) unsalted butter (room temperature)

7 oz (200 g) superfine sugar

2 large eggs (room temperature)

1 tsp vanilla extract

14 oz (400 g) all-purpose flour

½ tsp salt

Tip

If you find that the dough sticks to the rolling pin, put a piece of plastic wrap or parchment paper between the dough and the rolling pin. You can also add a little bit of flour to the dough if it is really sticky, but do so sparingly, since too much flour will make the dough tough.

Method

1. Using an electric mixer, cream the butter and superfine sugar together until pale and fluffy, then beat in the eggs one at a time, and then the vanilla extract. In another bowl, combine the flour and salt. Add the dry ingredients to the butter and eggs, and mix gently until well combined. You will probably find that the electric mixer struggles to combine all of the ingredients once the dry ingredients are added, so you may have to mix it all together with a spoon. Form the dough into a flattened disk and wrap it in plastic wrap before placing it in a refrigerator for at least an hour to firm up. Preheat the oven to 350°F (180°C/gas mark 4) while you are letting the dough rest.

2. Once the dough is ready to roll out, place it on a lightly floured surface and roll it out to the required thickness. Cut the dough into shapes, using cookie cutters or a knife. Carefully lift the cookies with a palette knife onto baking sheets lined with parchment paper. Be sure to place the cookies an inch or so apart on the sheets, so that they are not touching.

3. Bake the cookies for 8 to 12 minutes. You'll know they are ready when the edges just start turning golden. Don't worry if they are still soft in the middle—they will firm up as they cool. Transfer the cookies from the sheet to a wire rack with a palette knife. Wait until they have completely cooled before decorating.

Gingerbread

Ingredients *(makes about 24 cookies)*

4½ oz (125 g) unsalted butter (room temperature)
4 oz (110 g) dark brown sugar
1 large egg yolk (room temperature)
4 fl oz (125 ml) golden syrup
10 oz (280 g) all-purpose flour
3 tsp ground ginger
1 tsp mixed spice

Tips

Gingerbread cookies can be stored in an airtight container for up to 2 months.

✱

Try to make sure that all cookies on a baking sheet are approximately the same size to allow for an even bake.

✱

Using eggs and butter at room temperature will make baking easier. Leave the butter out of the refrigerator for about an hour beforehand and it will be soft enough to beat together with the sugar to achieve a pale, fluffy mixture. Cold eggs can cause the mixture to curdle. If this happens, you can rescue the mixture by vigorously mixing in a large tablespoon of all-purpose flour.

Method

1. Beat the butter, dark brown sugar, and egg yolk in a bowl with an electric mixer until smooth and all the ingredients are well combined.

2. Stir in the golden syrup, sifted flour, ginger and mixed spice in two batches to ensure all the ingredients are mixed together properly. If the dough is slightly crumbly, add a little more golden syrup.

3. Knead the dough on a floured surface, then wrap it in plastic wrap and allow it to firm in a refrigerator for at least an hour. Preheat the oven to 350°F (180°C/gas mark 4) while you are letting the dough rest.

4. Once the dough is ready to roll out, place it on a floured surface and roll it out to the required thickness. If you find that the dough sticks to the rolling pin, put a piece of plastic wrap or parchment paper between the dough and the rolling pin. Cut the dough into shapes, using cookie cutters or a knife. Carefully lift the cookies with a palette knife onto baking sheets lined with parchment paper. Be sure to place the cookies an inch or so apart on the sheets, so that they are not touching.

5. Bake the cookies for 12 to 15 minutes until they are lightly browned on the edges, before placing them on wire racks to cool. The cookies will harden as they cool.

Royal Icing

Royal icing is a firm-setting mixture of confectioners' sugar and egg white that can be used in a variety of ways, including decorating the surface of cookies, piping intricate decorations, and attaching edible decorations to cookies. It is important to keep royal icing covered, since it dries out quickly and will develop a crust on its surface, which will make it unsuitable for piping (the crust will block the decorating tip). To prevent a crust from forming, cover the surface of freshly made royal icing with a damp cloth and then plastic wrap. Royal icing can be stored for up to 5 days in an airtight container in a refrigerator, but it is important to remix it with a wooden spoon when it is needed to achieve the desired consistency. When making royal icing, always mix to a stiff-peak consistency, and then gradually add water, a teaspoon at a time, to achieve the desired consistency.

Ingredients (*Makes 8³/₄ oz [250 g] royal icing*)

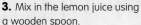

8½ oz (240 g) confectioners' sugar

1 large egg white

¼ tsp lemon juice

Method

1. Sift the confectioners' sugar into a bowl and add the egg white.

2. Mix together on a low speed using an electric mixer for about 5 minutes until the icing has a medium- to stiff-peak consistency.

3. Mix in the lemon juice using a wooden spoon.

Tips

Medium- and stiff-peak royal icing is often used for piping decorations.

Royal icing can also be thinned down to a liquid with a few drops of water to flood cookies (see page 18).

＊

When piping royal icing, how stiff you want to make the icing is a personal choice—but as a rule, if the icing dribbles out of the decorating tip by itself, it is too soft. Conversely, if you can't pipe without squeezing the piping bag so hard it is likely to split, then it is too stiff. A medium consistency is always a good starting point.

Fondant

Fondant, also known as rolled fondant, plastic icing, or ready-to-roll icing, is a sugar dough used to cover cookies and cakes and make edible decorations for your bakes. It has a relatively long shelf life and is readily available in supermarkets and cake-decorating supply stores in a range of colors. If you prefer not to use a commercial fondant, you can make your own, using the recipe shown here.

Ingredients *(makes 1 lb 2 oz [500 g] white fondant)*

1 lb 2 oz (500 g) confectioners' sugar, plus extra for dusting

2 tbsp liquid glucose

1 large egg white

Tips

Fondant will keep well for months if it is tightly wrapped in plastic wrap and stored at room temperature.

If your fondant becomes dry while you are working with it, white vegetable fat (shortening) can be kneaded into it to soften it.

Fondant is too soft for making delicate decorations, but adding CMC or Tylo powder will give it more strength and then it can be rolled more thinly.

Method

1. Sift the confectioners' sugar into a large bowl. Make a well in the center and slowly stir in the liquid glucose and egg white with a wooden spoon until the mixture is combined into a dough.

2. Place the fondant on a surface dusted with confectioners' sugar and knead until smooth and pliable. You may need to sprinkle the fondant with extra confectioners' sugar if it becomes too sticky. The fondant can be used immediately or wrapped tightly in plastic wrap and stored at room temperature until required.

Marshmallow Fondant

Fondant can also be made with marshmallows. Some people prefer using this type of fondant because it is softer and sweeter than regular fondant.

Tip

Don't store fondant-covered cookies or fondant decorations in the refrigerator—the fondant will absorb condensation and will wilt.

Ingredients (makes 1 lb 2 oz [500 g] white marshmallow fondant)

1 lb 2 oz (500 g) white mini marshmallows

2 tbsp water

White vegetable fat (shortening), for greasing

1 lb 4 oz (575 g) confectioners' sugar, sifted

Method

1. Place the mini marshmallows and water in a large microwave-proof bowl and then place the bowl in a microwave for 1 minute on a medium setting. Allow the mixture to rest for 1 minute, then microwave it again for another minute.

2. Remove the bowl from the microwave and then stir the mixture with a wooden spoon that has been greased with white vegetable fat (to prevent the mixture from sticking to it) until smooth.

3. Stir in the confectioners' sugar until well combined.

4. Knead the marshmallow fondant until smooth. Wrap it in plastic wrap and store at room temperature until required.

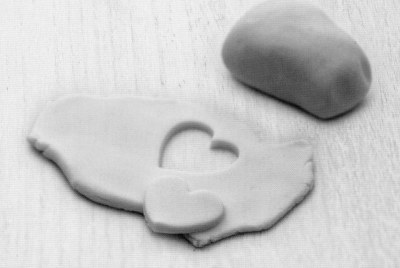

Templates

If you can't find a suitable cutter, you can make a template instead. Find an image that reflects the shape you want, and re-size it using a photocopier or computer. Trace the image onto tracing paper with a pen, and then cut it out with scissors. All the templates on these pages for the featured projects are shown at 100 percent.

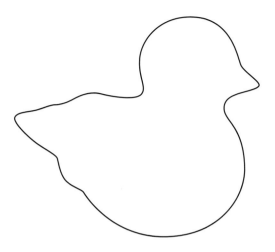

Bathtime Fun, page 28

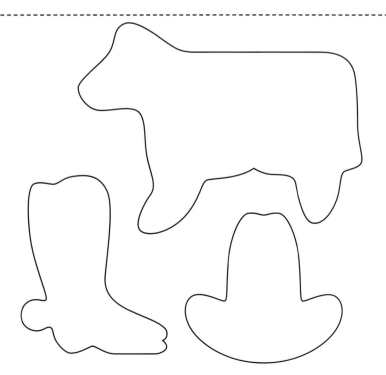

On the Ranch, page 52

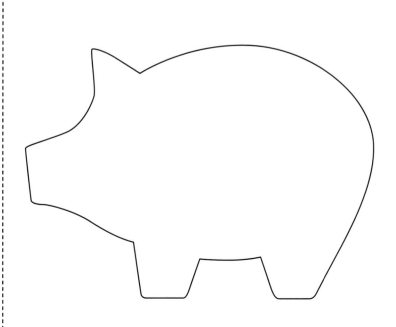

Piggy Banks, page 54

Teapot Delight, page 32

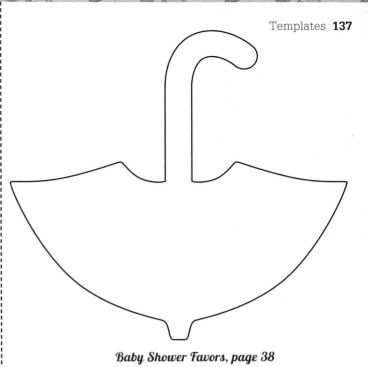

Baby Shower Favors, page 38

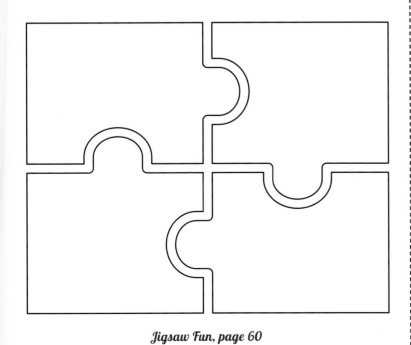

Jigsaw Fun, page 60

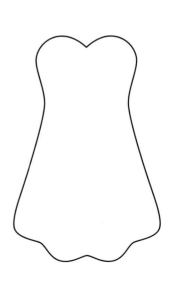

Party Dresses, page 62

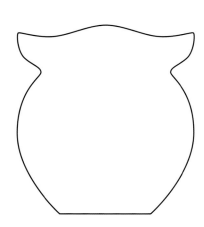

Gingham Owls, page 66

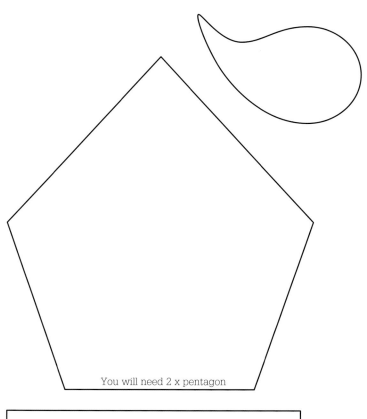

You will need 2 x pentagon

You will need
2 x rectangle

You will need 3 x square

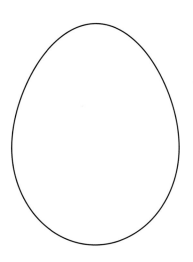

Ombré Ruffle Eggs, page 90

Birdhouse Beauties, page 80

Spring Bouquets, page 86

Teddy Bears, page 88

Charm Bracelets, page 94

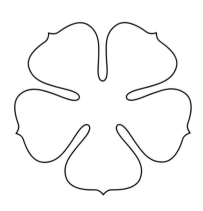

Marbled Flowers, page 96

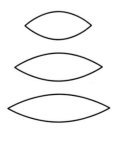

Whimsical Water Lilies, page 108

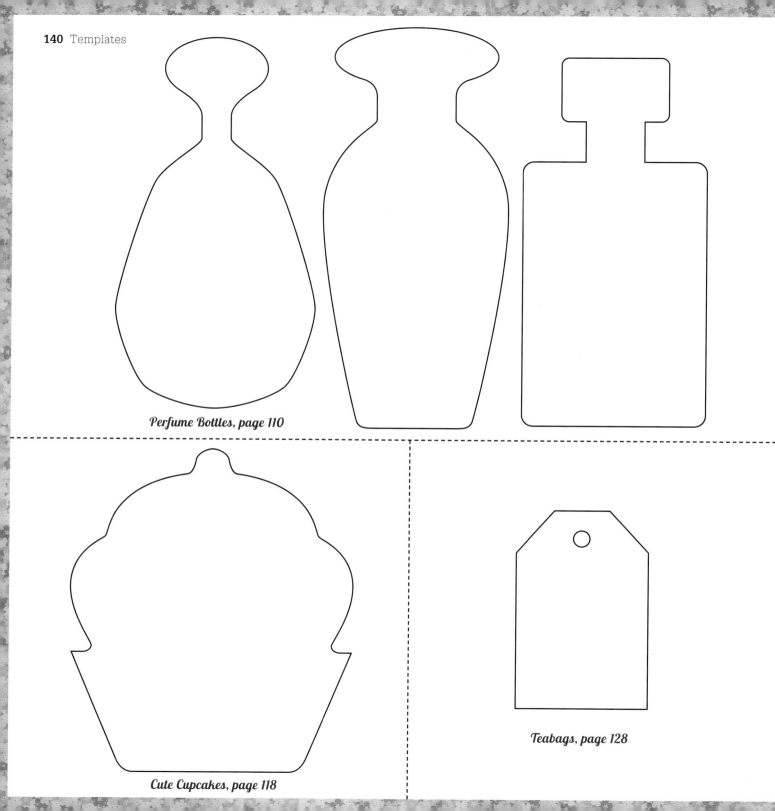

Perfume Bottles, page 110

Cute Cupcakes, page 118

Teabags, page 128

Here are some tips to help demystify baking jargon and show you how to avoid common problems that everyone experiences at some point during their cookie decorating journey.

Troubleshooting Q & A

Q **Help, my thinned royal icing is full of bubbles!**

A When adding water to royal icing to enable you to flood the surface of cookies (see page 18), air bubbles can form, which can burst while the icing is drying and leave craters in the surface of your cookie. To minimize the number of bubbles, stir in the water gently with a spatula, cover the bowl with a damp dish towel, and let the royal icing rest for at least 15 minutes. During this time, most of the bubbles will rise to the surface and pop. If you do see bubbles in your icing once you have flooded your cookie, pop them immediately with a pin or toothpick.

Q **I don't have a microwave. Is there another easy way to melt chocolate or candy wafers?**

A If you don't have a microwave, you can also melt chocolate or candy wafers in a heat-proof bowl set over a saucepan of simmering water. Add the chocolate to the bowl and stir until melted. Make sure the base of the bowl doesn't touch the water in the saucepan. The chocolate will be heated by the steam trapped in the saucepan. When you have finished, remove the bowl from the saucepan and dry the base before tipping the chocolate out, to ensure that water doesn't spill into the chocolate and spoil it.

Q **What is the difference between soft-, medium-, and stiff-peak royal icing?**

A Royal icing can be made in different consistencies—it can be thickened by adding extra confectioners' sugar, or thinned by adding extra water. "Stiff-peak" means that the royal icing will stand up on its own when a whisk is dipped into it and taken out again. This type of icing is hard to squeeze through a piping bag and is best used to attach three-dimensional cookies together or affix decorations to the surface of cookies. "Medium-peak" and "soft-peak" icing is most commonly used for piping decorations such as lines and dots. Royal icing mixed to a medium peak will be fluffy and have soft peaks with a curve. It is often described as having the consistency of toothpaste. Soft-peak icing will only just form peaks, but it is still firm enough that it won't dribble out of the end of a piping bag.

Q **Why is my fondant sweating?**

A Fondant can be affected by temperature and humidity. In warm or humid environments, it can become soft and sticky, making it difficult to work with. The surface of the fondant may also look shiny, like it is sweating. Unfortunately, if you work in a hot environment, it is difficult to avoid this problem unless you work in a temperature-controlled room. Adding cornstarch can help reduce the stickiness or you can also try to cool your hands before working with fondant. Also, once your fondant-covered cookies are complete, keep them in a cool, dark place to avoid them from spoiling before being served.

Note: If you do cool your hands under cold water, remember to dry them thoroughly before touching the fondant. Water and fondant don't mix. Water droplets will dissolve the sugar in the fondant, leaving small blemishes on the surface.

Q **Why are my cookies spreading while baking?**

A A little bit of spreading during baking is normal, but there are a few tips you can follow to ensure that your cookies keep their shape as much as possible:

✳ Omit any leavening agent (such as baking powder) from your cookie dough recipe.

✳ Be careful not to mix the butter and sugar for too long. Over-mixing can cause too much air to be incorporated.

✳ Freeze cut-out shapes for 5–10 minutes before baking.

✳ Cover your baking sheet with parchment paper rather than greasing it with any type of fat. Cookies tend to spread more when resting on a greasy surface.

Suppliers

USA

CopperGifts.com
www.coppergifts.com
900 N. 32nd Street
Parsons, KS 67357
Tel: +1 620 421 0654

Ecrandal
www.ecrandal.com
P.O. Box 7795
Flint, MI 48507

Fancy Flours
www.fancyflours.com
705 Osterman Drive, Suite E
Bozeman, MT 59715
Tel: +1 406 587 0118

Global Sugar Art
www.globalsugarart.com
1509 Military Turnpike
Plattsburgh, NY 12901
Tel: +1 518 561 3039

UK

Alphabet Moulds
www.alphabetmoulds.co.uk
16 Winston Road, Barry
Vale of Glamorgan, Wales, CF62 9SW
Tel: +44 (0)1446 420901

Cakeology Ltd
www.cakeology.net
582 Kingston Road
London, SW20 8DN
Tel: + 44 (0)20 8127 5166

Cakes Cookies and Crafts Shop
www.cakescookiesandcraftsshop.co.uk
Unit 12, Bowmans Trading Estate
Westmoreland Road
London, NW9 9RL
Tel: +44 (0)1524 389684

Cake Decorating Company
www.thecakedecoratingcompany.co.uk
Unit 2b Triumph Road
Nottingham, NG7 2GA
Tel: +44 (0)115 969 9800

Cake Stuff
www.cake-stuff.com
Milton Industrial Estate
Lesmahagow, Lanarkshire
Scotland, ML11 0JN
Tel: +44 (0)1555 890111

Lindy's Cakes Ltd
www.lindyscakes.co.uk
Unit 2, Station Approach
Wendover, Aylesbury
Buckinghamshire, HP22 6BN
Tel: + 44 (0)1296 622418

Squire's Kitchen Shop
www.squires-shop.com
3 Waverly Lane, Farnham
Surrey, GU9 8BB
Tel: +44 (0)845 617 1810

AUSTRALIA

Cake Deco
www.cakedeco.com.au
Shop 7, Port Phillip Arcade,
232 Flinders Street
Melbourne, Victoria 3000
Tel: +61 (0)3 9654 5335

Cakes Around Town
www.cakesaroundtown.com.au
Unit 2/12 Sudbury Street
Darra, Brisbane, Queensland 4076
Tel: +61 (0)7 3160 8728

Cake Decorating Solutions
www.cakedecoratingsolutions.com.au
311 Penshurst Street
Willoughby, New South Wales 2068
Tel: + 61 (0)2 9417 5666

Tip

Etsy and Ebay also have lovely cookie cutters, decorating equipment, and silicone molds.

Index

Author's Acknowledgments

This book has been such a pleasure to create and I would like to thank everyone who has made it possible. It has been a huge team effort and I could not have done it without the help of the following people:

Many thanks to the team at Quarto Publishing—especially Kate Kirby, Moira Clinch, Karin Skånberg, Ruth Patrick, and Caroline Guest—for their wealth of fabulous advice and support in turning my initial ideas into such a fun book. A huge thank you also to my wonderful photographer Sian Irvine and her assistant Joe Giacomet, who worked incredibly hard to capture all of the technique steps and cookies so beautifully.

Thanks also to Jenni from Hip Hop Hooray, for designing such a lovely vintage picture for the jigsaw cookie project on page 60.

As always, I am incredibly grateful for the constant support of my family and friends. In particular, a massive thank you to my husband Dave, for his never-ending patience while I took over the kitchen experimenting with new recipes and designs; for not complaining about the mess and the constant cloud of icing sugar on everything; and for always giving me honest, useful advice to help me take my baking and designs to the next level.

Publisher's Acknowledgements

All step-by-step and other images are the copyright of Quarto Publishing plc. While every effort has been made to credit contributors, Quarto would like to apologize should there have been any omissions or errors—and would be pleased to make the appropriate corrections for future editions of the book.